IMAGES
of America

ASBURY PARK
A CENTURY OF CHANGE

ASBURY PARK

PUBLISHED BY GREATER ASBURY PARK CHAMBER OF COMMERCE · 1975-76

With a "mod" cover design by Barnes & Kenney ("effective communication . . . by design") at 601 Bangs Avenue, the Greater Asbury Park Chamber of Commerce printed this guide book for 1975–1976. City hall was listed at 710 Bangs Avenue. Ray Kramer was mayor, and councilmen were Ascenzio R. Albarelli, Benjamin Edelstein, Edward R. English, and Dr. Lorenzo Harris. William J. Shiel was city manager, with Norman Mesnikoff attorney and Mary Vacarro Martin city clerk. William Bruno was the beachfront director, and Thomas Smith was the police chief. (Author's collection.)

ON THE COVER: Coast Cities Coaches, which operated out of Neptune, was launched by Denis Gallagher Jr., who was originally from Passaic. (Author's collection.)

IMAGES
of America

ASBURY PARK
A CENTURY OF CHANGE

Helen-Chantal Pike

ARCADIA
PUBLISHING

Published by Arcadia Publishing
Charleston, South Carolina

Printed in the United States of America

Library of Congress Control Number: 2020938307

For all general information, please contact Arcadia Publishing:
Telephone 843-853-2070
Fax 843-853-0044
E-mail sales@arcadiapublishing.com
For customer service and orders:
Toll-Free 1-888-313-2665

Visit us on the Internet at www.arcadiapublishing.com

In memory of Joan L. Culloo McLaughlin Flatley.
Jersey City's loss was Asbury's Park's gain.
Thanks for the stories, the insights, and especially the laughter.

CONTENTS

Acknowledgments

Asbury Park: A Century of Change came to fruition with the help of several individuals who share my curiosity and determination to gather history, much of which has not remained static in the midst of extraordinary 21st-century changes. Steve Albert and Susan L. Rosenberg, thank you.

Gratitude also goes to photographers Debra L. Rothenberg, Kristen Driscoll, Mike McLaughlin, Dave Christopher, Gary Crawford, Davis Duzit, Lisa Carlson, Sue Peckman, and Hoag Levins, who honored my "Hail Mary" request. To Rita Marano, George A. Kary, Steve Eccles, and Rickey Stein, thanks for helping me make it across the finish line.

A special thank-you to Pasqualina DeLucia DeBoer, marketing director of Madison Marquette; genealogist Shelley Farnham Hiber; and Steve and Kathy Bumball for your hospitality.

Spelunking with me into the past was realtor David Dorfman, with whom I share a connection to Monmouth College, where both our fathers were professors. It's also where the late Rainette Bannister Holiman studied French with my father; I am grateful I could introduce her to muralist Bob Mataranglo. Thanks to Beth Ann Duze Woolley for coming along when I needed a Jewish mother the most. *I'll Sleep When I'm Dead* is another project waiting for us.

After too many decades to count, a special shout-out goes to Daniel Dorn Jr. for the most memorable plane ride ever back in 1998. Flying out of Allaire Airport in Wall Township spawned more adventures and a different Asbury Park book that would have to include the late Ed Brown.

For all the conversations we have had—and hope we continue to have—thank you to fellow author, photographer, and astute observer of humankind Madonna Carter Jackson.

I also wish to thank Caroline Anderson at Arcadia Publishing for her forbearance.

Now a word about how to use this book: each of the first four chapters covers a compass point and opens with a map that melds together a post–World War II Asbury Park with the second decade of the 21st century. The orientation is west to east, the approach many take to get to Shangri-la. Enjoy the journey.

INTRODUCTION

In the decades following the end of World War I in 1918, Asbury Park regained its momentum as a popular—and expanding—residential resort on the Atlantic Coast. Officially incorporated in 1871, Asbury Park offered a lot to travelers searching for a seaside destination to refresh their hardworking sensibilities. To young families looking to put down roots, the lure of an up-and-coming coastal community midway between New York and Philadelphia was undeniable.

From the Roaring Twenties, through women's suffrage, Prohibition, the Great Depression, World II, and the suburbanization of Monmouth County farmland, this city-by-the-sea experienced a series of economic cycles fueled in no small part by the rivalry between rail travel and personal vehicles that changed its carefully thought-out 19th-century landscape.

The last undeveloped parcel of land west of Main Street, north of Asbury Avenue and overlooking Deal Lake, changed dramatically in the 20th century. Early newspaper accounts described an idyllic forest, attractive for summer camping. But as more all-season residents moved in, the natural resource was turned into construction lumber and heating fuel. The most notable change was the building of a million-dollar high school and football stadium overlooking the lakefront. Its construction in 1926 moved this important civic function from its original, and cramped, east side location on Bond Street to a more spacious and modern campus west of Main, where most of Asbury Park's year-round, working families were living.

As the 21st century rolls on, new changes are in store—none more dramatic than the lifting of a decades-long embargo on development of its prized oceanfront. Real estate development—both commercial and civic—is building a new look for Asbury Park.

In an ironic echo of founder James A. Bradley's early strategy of placing historical relics on the waterfront, Asbury Park's history is found all over this jewel of a city. Turn the pages to discover how the past lives with the present, and may yet shape the future.

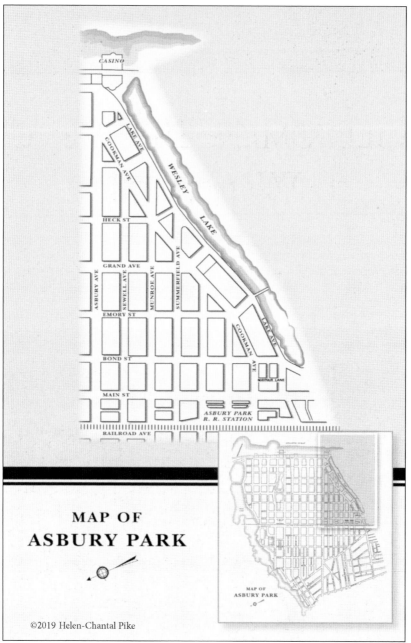

MAP OF
ASBURY PARK

©2019 Helen-Chantal Pike

Nothing transformed travel like the automobile, which guaranteed a door-to-door experience like nothing before. As cars became ever more affordable, roads were paved to bring vacationers and shoppers as close to their destinations as possible. This c. 1971 map shows the streets in the central business district (CBD) during the mid-20th century. In a nod to history and the need for stronger locators for emergency calls, city hall named all the alleys in 2018. Mayfair Lane in the CBD pays homage to the movie palace designed by theater architect Thomas Lamb on the corner of Lake Avenue and St. James Place. In 2014, the CBD was listed in the National Register of Historic Places—a good first step for any municipality looking to draft preservation guidelines. (Map by author.)

One

WILLKOMEN, BIENVENUE, WELCOME!

Coming to Asbury Park in the 1920s still meant arriving by train for most. After pressuring the New York & Long Branch Railroad for a modern depot to handle the swell in visitors, Asbury Park got a second station that opened on November 2, 1922. Coast Cities Buses were operated by the Gallagher family out of Neptune. But as cars overtook the trains, the station's six ticket windows dwindled to one. Conrail, the depot's next owner, was looking to unload underperforming stations and offered it to the city. In March 1978, it was torn down to make way for parking and a much-needed municipal complex from Bangs Avenue south to Cookman Avenue. (Author's collection.)

Who could have predicted the third station, occupying land from Cookman Avenue south to Springwood Avenue, would also serve as a public space for performances and the city's cultural artifacts? In 2011, the first artwork to be hung was "Tree of Life" by Cuban artist Josignacio. (Author's collection.)

In September 2016, mixed-media artist Patty Arroyo pauses to visit with her son Sid Morris while painting the mural she designed for the underground walkway that connects the north and south platforms. (Courtesy of Patty Arroyo.)

The Asbury Park Historical Society rescued the Rainbow Room nightclub sign from the Albion Hotel on Second Avenue at Ocean Avenue before it was torn down. The sign is also a symbolic hat-tip to the city's vibrant lesbian and gay culture and the three businesswomen—Carol Torre, Camille Neto, and Kay SanFillippo—who, from 1981 to 1989, operated the historic property as the Key West Hotel, retaining the Rainbow Room as a downstairs dance club while upstairs was the disco Over the Rainbow. The wooden bench likely came from either the original Queen Anne Victorian station or the North Asbury Park station at Fifth Avenue. (Author's collection.)

After World War II, the *Asbury Park Press* grew in circulation to rival the *Star-Ledger* in Newark as the second-largest daily in the state. But in the pre-diesel days, when horses were the engines and the North Jersey Shore largely a resort region, the *Press* was delivered in this wagon for bulk distribution to hotel lobbies, tobacconists, grocery stores, and even other train stations. The newspaper donated it to the historical society in 2014. (Author's collection.)

Train visitors were once greeted by two rival department stores on opposing Main Street and Cookman Avenue corners. Cook's Beehive closed in 1929. A variety of businesses were housed here until the one with history relocated from Allenhurst, the Conover Real Estate Agency. Started in 1906 by John Conover, the son-in-law of Asbury Park's well-digger Uriah White, in 2018, the firm joined the global real estate network Berkshire Hathaway. (Author's collection.)

Every now and again, the streets are opened up for utility work, revealing the tracks of the Seashore Electric Railway Company, started in 1888 and seen here in 1998 in front of the old Cook's Beehive. The original circuit followed Cookman Avenue to Kingsley Street, then turned north to Eighth Avenue, west to Emory Street, south over Sunset Lake to Asbury Avenue, west to Main Street, and then south either to Bangs Avenue, where it turned into the train station parking lot, or to Cookman. Electric rail service stopped in 1931. (Author's collection.)

Henry Steinbach had the competing store. It burned in 1915, and the lot remained empty until the next century. The Environmental and Shade Tree Commission, under chair Tom Pivinski (far right), with dedicated volunteers, turned it into Merchants Park with the help of Steven Botta, chef-owner of Brando's Citi Cucina next door. The park is one of sixteen the commission maintains. (Courtesy of Sue Peckman.)

The building south of Merchants Park held a number of businesses from furniture stores to the Owl and the Pussycat Bar. In the new century, Insano's was a short-lived restaurant with a handsomely carved bar rescued from the teardown of a 19th-century oyster bar on Bond Street that in the later 20th century was Matty's Bar, popular with *Asbury Park Press* employees. Steven Botta opened his Italian restaurant here in 2011. (Courtesy of Susan L. Rosenberg.)

An early morning explosion at the Glamour Girl Beauty Lounge on Thursday, May 28, 1964, destroyed three buildings and six stores and caused one fatality. Lost were the Music Center, Asbury Flowerland, McNaughton's Restaurant, Henry Marton Jewelers, and Goldstein's Stationery Store & Luncheonette—all in buildings erected in 1881. Never rebuilt, the empty lot was used for extra parking for decades. It is now the expansion of Johnny Mac's House of Spirits, the original office location for 19th-century realtor Milan Ross. (Author's collection.)

Artist Isaiah Zagar created Philadelphia's Magic Gardens, an immersive mixed-media art environment completely covered with mosaics. Cookman Avenue gallery owner Kate Mellina commissioned him to create a colorful mosaic of tile and mirrors for the west side of her building that could be seen from Main Street. Reconstruction of surrounding buildings has shaken loose much of Zagar's creation, and only patches remain visible in 2020. (Author's collection.)

Realtor T. Frank Appleby built a distinctive brick and terra-cotta office on the southeast corner of Main Street and Mattison Avenue in 1922, replacing a wood-frame building erected by James A. Bradley. It was part of the CBD application to the National Register of Historic Places with other buildings whose original architectural style had remained intact for nearly 100 years. It was torn down in the summer of 2019, slated to be rebuilt with the same design. Its last commercial use was as the hugely popular Spanish-Portuguese restaurant Bistro Ole. (Author's collection.)

The discovery of clay deposits in New Jersey spawned an entire industry of tile, as useful as it was decorative. A lot of it centered in the Raritan Valley around Sayreville, South River, and South Amboy, with sales offices in Asbury Park. In 1998, this was what remained of the only tiled street sign in the CBD at the southeast corner of Main Street. (Author's collection.)

One of the first Asbury Park buildings listed in the National Register of Historic Places (in 1979) was a two-story brick edifice with Italianate design built by Henry C. Winsor, president of the Asbury Park–Ocean Grove Bank (now Santander). Winsor died in 1922. The building was erected in 1904 and succeeded two previous wood-frame buildings that burned. In 2019, artist Patty Arroyo opened a gallery in one of the storefronts. (Author's collection.)

More than 30 years ago, Sebastian "Sam" Vaccaro opened the Hardware Store of Asbury Park in the former location of the H.R. Ingalls dealership for Buicks and Cadillacs on the southeast corner of Main Street and Summerfield Avenue. As the third generation of his family with deep roots in the city, Sam—and his staff's—knowledge of the needs of its historic buildings is a valuable resource for new homeowners looking to restore the gems that make the city distinctive among the shore's residential resorts. (Both, author's collection.)

Popular with World War II and Vietnam veterans, among others, the Clover Club was on the northwest corner of Main Street and Monroe Avenue. It retains its original neon sign on the exterior, but inside is Asbury Park's longest-running music incubator. (Author's collection.)

Seen here with singer-songwriter Kevin John Allen (left), Rutgers University radio DJ Scott Stamper has, since November 1994, continuously run the Saint. The intimate performance space is known for showcasing rising talent, acoustic sets, and serving as a recording studio for live concerts. With Peter Mantas, Stamper co-founded the annual Asbury Park Music Awards. (Courtesy of Davis Duzit.)

In 2008, German Garcia took an unassuming bodega on Main Street at Sewell Avenue and turned several connected storefronts into Plaza Tapatía, a specialty grocery store, taqueria, liquor store, bar, and restaurant whose name takes its inspiration from his hometown of Guadalajara, Mexico. His culinary neighbors include TJ's Pizza, which opened in 1982, and Lucky Star Chinese. (Courtesy of Susan L. Rosenberg.)

Veterans of Foreign Wars Harold Daley Post No. 1333 met at 708 Main Street, between Sewall and Asbury Avenues. In 1965, it paid $47,100 to buy the National Guard Armory on Lake Avenue and Bond Street after the guard had moved out in 1961. (Author's collection.)

In 1942, John F. Foley decided to trade in Foley's Grill on the west side of Main Street for a diner across the street, on the southeast corner of Asbury Avenue. It was the perfect location for beachgoers coming into the city and patrons exiting bars at 2:00 a.m. (or later). The property was sold to make way for a CVS pharmacy and then sold again for its current use as a satellite of the Monmouth County prosecutor's office. (Author's collection.)

In May 1948, N.Y. & N.J. Cleaners and Dyers bought out Maurice Gallus, who, with his brother, Emmanuel, had taken over their father's dry cleaning and dye operation, moving the Sanitary Steam Press at 416 Bond Street to Asbury Avenue east of Railroad Avenue. The brothers went into a new business, Atlantic Appliances, at 711–715 Main Street, with partner Murry Connors of Deal. Currently, it is the warehouse for Flux Modern, the mid-century modern furniture store on Cookman Avenue in the "red-front" F.W. Woolworth building. (Author's collection.)

Returning to the Central Business District core in the 700 block of Cookman Avenue, Cleopatra Steps Out was a fiber gallery ahead of its time. It became the unofficial headquarters for the 1990s renaissance, thanks to owner and later councilwoman Kate Mellina, seen here with her husband, photographer Dave Christopher (center) and the late Chris Flynn, who worked tirelessly to try to save the Palace Amusements. They hold an iconic painting by artist Patti Kaufman. In 2006, Kate and Dave relocated to Philadelphia, and Kate sold the building to Malcolm Navias of Studebaker's, who gave the building a modern makeover into Heaven Art & Antiques. (Author's collection.)

Paying tribute to the late Joe Harvard in March 2019 are, from left to right, musician Don Haynie, Kristen Driscoll and John Paul Alfonso, Shannon Barry, Harvard (in framed portrait), musician Rick Barry, Harvard's longtime partner Mallory Massara, co-owner of the Parlor Gallery Jenn Hampton, and musician and LGBT activist Geena Alessia Buono. An accomplished musician, producer, and artist, Harvard cultivated the gARTen, an outdoor gallery of "trash art" and a music gathering place in this vacant lot between Parlor and the former C Jay's. (Courtesy of Kristen Driscoll Photography.)

In May 1964, Cynthia Joy and Jerry Hirshenson opened C Jay's Record Store. A teenaged Southside Johnny Lyon bought the latest albums to share with other coming-of-age musicians. Fellow Ocean Grove native Shep Pettibone worked his way up to buyer and manager before leaving for New York to make his mark working with Madonna. In 1973, Bruce Springsteen did an in-store signing of his first album, *Greetings From Asbury Park*. The store closed in 1983. (Author's collection.)

The city's first new movie house in decades, The ShowRoom originally opened on the southside of Cookman Avenue as a storefront art house theater in 2009. The one-time home of Parke Drugs, the property is now home to Catsbury Park, a tea house and cat lounge opened by Bouncing Souls' stage manager D.J. Bornschien in 2017. (Author's collection.)

Corporate meeting producers Mike Sodano and Nancy Sabino moved from north Jersey and eventually bought the property across Cookman Avenue to launch The ShowRoom Cinema in the former space occupied by the fashion designer Bird. The couple also makes videos for local projects, charities, and individuals. They expanded by acquiring the independent movie house in Bradley Beach, James A. Bradley's other seaside development, in 2018. (Author's collection.)

Veteran concert promoter Tony Pallagrosi, with business partner Kevin Lyman, brought the Vans WARP Tour to outdoor stages at the former Mrs. Jay's Beer Garden next to the Stone Pony and in the Berkeley Hotel's parking lot. They began in 1995 with 3,200 teenaged fans. The last tour stop in 2003 brought in 17,000. During the 2011 Asbury Park: Where Music Lives, Pallagrosi spoke about music's ability to bring audiences to Asbury Park, even in the cold winter months. (Author's collection/Kristen Driscoll Photography.)

In the 21st century, it is difficult to envision Cookman Avenue crossing Main Street, the railroad tracks, and going on for two more blocks before ending at Prospect Avenue. But Cookman was one of the original streets connecting the east and west sides. (Courtesy of Jeff Lundenberger.)

This rare winter scene of the southwest corner of Cookman Avenue and Main Street shows the spacious second location of Bob & Irving, a menswear store. Partners Robert Kamber and Irving Segan started out around the corner on Main in a much narrower store. Most of the site today is the train station's parking lot and a rain garden maintained by the Environmental and Shade Tree Commission designed to filter stormwater runoff. (Author's collection.)

Howard Borden's former clothing store was briefly home to Michelle Schaeffer's Be Gallery in the 1990s renaissance. It underwent a significant makeover in 2009 when Manhattanites Scott Hamm and Gene Mignola took possession. They transformed the space into a textile printing studio for costumes and interior design and a versatile décor store, Shelter Home, run by Hamm, who was a fashion model in Paris and Milan. He opened a souvenir-themed store on the boardwalk called the Asbury Park Fun House. In June 2020, Hamm renamed Shelter Home Fun House and switched to selling Asbury Park–inspired merchandise. (Author's collection.)

John and Bess McCarthy were among the 1990s pioneers, buying two vacant storefronts on the northwest corner of Cookman Avenue and Bond Street. They opened Ocean Park Gallery in 1997, a picture framing and prints store that is still open for business as the 21st century—and the city's renaissance—continues to unfold. (Author's collection.)

Real estate developer Pat Fasano bought a former lesbian bar, and in 2009 turned it into a down-home, affordable burger and beer joint he called Bond Street Bar. (Author's collection.)

Fasano, formerly of New Brunswick, and his frequent real estate partner Pat Schiavino, formerly of Montclair, were part of the 1990s renaissance, partnering to buy properties. Using old postcards, Fasano set about recreating the look of early-20th-century buildings east of painter Schiavino's art629 gallery. (Author's collection.)

With a degree in industrial art and interior design, plus a stint as the Club Bene talent booker in Sayreville, in 2006, Schiavino launched Asbury Underground, a downtown "crawl" of artists' work on display in participating venues. Over the years, this annual fall festival has grown to include music, expanded to three weeks, and now also occurs in January during the annual Light of Day concert series. (Courtesy of Susan L. Rosenberg.)

Researching claims of the supernatural for over 20 years, Kathy Kelley opened Paranormal Books & Curiosities in 2008, leading downtown walking tours and organizing public events. She is pictured in 2019 outside her shop, whose entrance retains the 1920s Abrams store name in the terrazzo tile. The Paranormal Museum's entrance is on the building's north side on Mattison Avenue. (Author's collection.)

Once dubbed Variety Store Row, Cookman Avenue's south side featured a series of five-and-dimes that followed the lead established by F.W. Woolworth. Real estate developer George Keator Fredericks built a mid-century modern building to keep J.J. Newberry Co. on Cookman Avenue in the 1950s. (Author's collection.)

This view of the 600 block of Lake Avenue in August 1955 includes McCrory's dime store (light building left of center). The imposing Victorian mansion at far left was the home of Uriah White. It was replaced with a parking lot owned by the VFW. A corner hutch and a carriage stone chiseled with "White" were moved to a descendant's home on Cedar Avenue in West Long Branch. (Author's collection.)

Many of the downtown streets were laid out following the curves in Wesley Lake, coming to points instead of traditional right-angled intersections. The most well-known came to be called Press Plaza. This 2003 view shows the extraordinary lengths developer Pat Fasano went to to rebuild the point of Cookman and Mattison Avenues. (Author's collection.)

Press Plaza includes the north-south Emory Street (out of view to the right). The north side of Mattison Avenue's eastern end, seen here, featured the original post office, the one-time *Asbury Park Press* building, and the c. 1950s location of the Salvation Army. The newspaper moved out of its namesake city and west to Neptune in 1986. (Author's collection.)

Inspired by British playwright Christopher Marlowe, Don Stine operated Antic Hay Books in a number of locations since May 1977, including the former second-floor newsroom of the *Asbury Park Press*. Stine hosted various events in that space with no windows, including a 2002 return of fortune teller Madame Marie who had left the boardwalk for a storefront on Highway 35 in Ocean Township during the oceanfront redevelopment's tumultuous years. (Author's collection.)

In 2000, Terri Thomas and a cadre of talented volunteers launched the Black Box with a mission to revitalize the empty storefronts and underutilized public places as arts incubators for film, poetry, LGBT programs, classical music, and theater. In 2002, Thomas initiated the Women's Arts Festival. Seated on the piano, she is seen here with her singing partner, Amy Giinther Fredericks; they were known as the Cadenzo Duo. Both Fredericks and her husband, Bruce Keator Fredericks (grandson of Dr. Bruce S. Keator, property developer and Asbury Park mayor), both passed in 2018. A professional opera singer who also taught voice to students at Westminster Choir College in Princeton, Thomas eventually took her experiences to the Monmouth County Arts Council and then to the Pacific Northwest. (Photograph by Paul Newland, courtesy of Terri Thomas.)

Director George Hansel oversees a rehearsal of *Chess*, a play written by 16-year-old Justin Sirios of Ocean Grove. It was part of the Black Box's inaugural Teen Arts Festival in 2004. The performance took place in Sulli Studios, a second-floor gallery overlooking Mattison and in the former *Asbury Park Press* editor's office. Collaborative artist Kelly Sullivan subsequently relocated to Lambertville, and Hansel moved to Holland. (Photograph by Paul Newland, courtesy of Terri Thomas.)

New York graphic designer Michael Liberatore is credited with writing the game-changing article about the affordable alternative to Fire Island and the Hamptons in the gay lifestyle magazine *Empire*. Published in 2000, his words brought in new pioneers who restored long-neglected homes and launched new businesses; for Liberatore, it was the Insomnia Café on Mattison. Another new pioneer was Joe D'Andrea, who became the lead advocate for the growing gay community. Sadly, both D'Andrea and Liberatore are no longer with us. (Author's collection.)

This vintage postcard view of the 600 block of Mattison Avenue shows Jackson's Market, which sold fresh produce including rhubarb, Jersey asparagus, and Baldwin apples by the basket, while the second floor housed simple apartments for the city's working class. Sometime after World War II, this was the address for the Press Box luncheonette, where one could order "Adam and Eve on a raft." DJ's Delights currently occupies the location where Insomnia was. Nearby is the door to the Paranormal Museum. (Author's collection.)

On July 15, 1927, Evelyn Cohen started work as the city's first female police officer. (Author's collection.)

On July 5, 1970, the day after the civil disturbance that erupted on the West Side, residents such as Kenny Wilson (center) could be found on the sidewalk in front of the police station/city hall at 710 Bangs Avenue (with a separate front entrance on Mattison Avenue). It would be another decade before overcrowded conditions finally led to a new municipal complex on Main Street. (Author's collection.)

Like his father before him (see chapter four), Dr. Lorenzo Harris Jr. ran for office. The year was 1957. It was a crowded slate. He did not win. But he did in 1973, becoming the first African American elected to office in Asbury Park. Harris served until 1985 and was instrumental in the development of the new municipal building and transportation center on Main Street. In 1993, his daughter Sharon won a seat on the city council. (Author's collection.)

Running as an independent, Dr. Henry Vaccaro (left) won a seat on the city council in 1957, becoming the first Italian American to retained the family surname and be elected. As fate would have it, he joined two other Georgetown University alums who also won election to the city council that May: Thomas Shebell and Joseph Mattice, both lawyers. Congratulating him is his brother, Dr. Sebastian Vaccaro. (Courtesy of Henry Vacarro Sr.)

This family portrait shows, from left to right, (first row) Dolly Shiel, Bill Shiel, and Mary Shiel Damato; (second row) Eileen Shiel Chapman, Mary S. Tonacchio, Joan S. Sanfilippo, and Cissie S. Maffia. Bill Shiel was city manager from 1970 to 1977, and was honored as "Man of the Year" in 1974. In May 2016, his daughter Eileen Shiel Chapman was appointed to fill a vacant seat on city council and then elected that November in the city's first election since changing to staggered terms. (Courtesy of Eileen S. Chapman.)

In 1893, the Asbury Park Wheelmen built a clubhouse in the 700 block of Bangs Avenue on the north side, for an estimated cost of $5,000. The upper floors were for "the ladies" and included a hall with a balcony. The lower floors had rooms for smoking, billiards, reading, and presumably dining, as there was a kitchen. In the basement was a bowling alley. Seen at right in 1998, the building was converted to law offices. (Author's collection.)

Kerri Martin carried on the original spirit of the Asbury Park Wheelmen when she opened Second Life Bikes. She started the nonprofit in 2006 in a Holy Spirit Church garage on Second Avenue, east of Main Street. After September 11, 2001, the avid cyclist switched from investment banking to a career with more personal meaning: a bike-earning program for children, plus affordable bike sales and repairs. She relocated to South Main Street within the former brick structure of the old Rialto Theater. (Author's collection.)

East of the club on Bangs Avenue was the Blue Note, a popular jazz club in the 1960s that owners Norma Keating and Matt Mattlin (seen here at piano) made into a comfortable gathering place for a growing gay clientele. Performing with Mattlin, from left to right, are Gil Schiavino, Marty Weiss, and Myron Lee Bove. This photograph is from the September 5, 1959, issue of *Spotlight* magazine. (Author's collection.)

The Blue Note was next door to Tusting's music store. Robert A. Tusting, one of the founding members of the Asbury Park Rotary Club, bought the music instrument business of William Baldwin and established a store on the northwest corner of Bangs Avenue and Bond Street. Both landmarks were replaced by the Mercury, residential condos built around 2007. (Author's collection.)

Baltimore-born World War II Army veteran Milton Edelman first came to Asbury Park in 1948 and worked at the Metropolitan Hotel on Asbury Avenue. After a stint in Texas, he returned and was the Monterey Hotel lens man when it closed in 1961 on Ocean Avenue. While Edelman had studios in Ocean Township and Neptune whenever he was in Asbury Park, he always had his camera with him, documenting the people and changes in Asbury Park, including this state office building dedication. He died in 2017 at the age of 94. (Author's collection.)

The Assemblyman Thomas Smith Asbury Park State Office Building on Bangs Avenue was dedicated in 2001 in memory of the city's former police chief and its first African American mayor. It replaced several buildings on Bangs Avenue and Bond Street, including Matty's Bar. (Courtesy of Steve Albert.)

When it opened in 1927, the 11-story office building on the northwest corner of Bangs Avenue and Emory Street was the Jersey Shore's tallest skyscraper, changing the scale of buildings in the Central Business District forever while bringing new parking challenges to the CBD. Jersey Shore weather battered the Indiana limestone frieze decorating the top floor. (The retail businesses in the foreground were demolished to make way for the Asbury Park National Bank and Trust Company's expansion in 1953, including parking.) Built by the electric company, the ground floor of 601 Bangs Avenue featured a two-story showroom that is the current location of the French brasserie Pascal & Sabine. Before its more recent conversion to a mixed-use residential and office building, business tenants in the 1990s were an interesting assortment of long-established lawyers, dentists, and a new rising entrepreneurial class that included the short-lived Asbury Park Consortium, marketing consultant and playwright Midge Guerra, and the Smith Group, which now owns the Art Deco beauty. It was also the original address of WYGG 88.1 FM—Radio Bonne Nouvelle (French for "Good News Radio"), the religious station serving the city's growing Haitian population. The station received a vital donation from Abner Louima, the Haitian immigrant brutally attacked by New York police in 1997 and whose subsequent settlement enabled him to make quiet philanthropic donations. Doris Spinks hosted a weekly gospel radio show from here. Print journalist Ron Holland rented air time and hosted *Let's Talk News*, a weekly public affairs show, for four years before moving to Charlotte, North Carolina, in 2005. (Author's collection.)

Financial journalist Maureen Nevin booked air time on WYGG for a Thursday night program, which started out as *Restore by the Shore* in July 2000; by November 2006, it was known as Asbury Radio. She curated a must-listen-to show of interviews with politicians, developers, musicians, writers, new business owners, and playwrights, a passion of hers that resulted in her two-act TV sitcom about real estate redevelopment, *Ocean Mile: The Deal.* For this c. 2002 Fourth of July parade, Nevin, left, promotes her program with the help of one-time café owner Sharon Gansoian of Maxine's on Mattison. (Courtesy of Maureen Nevin.)

In 1999, journalist-turned-lawyer-turned-newspaper publisher Dan Jacobson launched the *TriCity News*, a free, alternative weekly covering politics and art in Asbury Park, Long Branch, and Red Bank. In 2012, he launched the hyper-local online-only *Asbury Park Sun* in a historical nod to theater mogul Walter Reade Sr.'s two-year muckraking paper, which was produced in the former National Bank Building on the northeast corner of Mattison Avenue and Bond Street. (Author's collection.)

The Steinbach brothers erected a modest two-story redbrick building of retail and second-floor offices on the north side of Bangs Avenue at Emory Street partly to conceal the power plant for their department store. This property saw a wide variety of ground-floor businesses from a Christian Science Reading Room to El Lobo Negro Art Gallery run by John Brown and Doris Spinks. On Friday nights, the pair put on intimate jazz shows with such musicians as Dee Holland, Dorian Parreott, New Horizon, and the Paradox Jazz Ensemble. (Author's collection.)

In the summer of 2005, Brown and Spinks also hosted a night of spoken word performances that included mystery author Persia Walker of New York, performer Lorraine Stone of Eatontown, and memoirist Rainette Holimon of Asbury Park. (Author's collection.)

In 1921, department store patriarch John Steinbach bought the rest of the triangular-shaped block formed where Bangs and Cookman Avenues come to a point and extended his business, making the downtown a viable winter destination. This yellow-brick building with its classical design elements by architect Robert Cleverdon was the centerpiece in an ambitious downtown revitalization plan by Henry Vaccaro, who proposed a type of marketplace like Boston's Faneuil Hall to lure shoppers back from the suburban malls proliferating outside of Asbury Park. In 2007, developer Carter Sackman converted the upper floors to rental lofts, put a penthouse on the top floor, and signed leases for retail space on all three sidewalks. (Author's collection.)

Kennedy Park marks the eastern end of the Central Business District. This bronze bust of Pres. John F. Kennedy was created by Interlaken sculptor Fritz Cleary. After its exhibit at the 1964 Democratic National Convention in Atlantic City, it was installed here by the Asbury Park Lions Club. Cleary studied sculpting with Charles Keck at the National Academy of Design and also attended the Beaux-Arts Institute of Design, both in New York. Discharged from the Army in 1946, the Long Island native found his way to the Jersey Shore, where he started a 26-year career at the *Asbury Park Press* as a reporter, photographer, editor, and art critic. He died in 1993 at the age of 80. (Author's collection.)

Cleary and his wife, watercolorist Hope Harris Kielland, managed the Asbury Park Society of Fine Arts, its museum, and numerous exhibitions around the Jersey Shore from their gallery on Grand Avenue. Earlier in its history, the building had been the medical offices of Dr. James F. Ackerman (see chapter two). One house north of the First Avenue corner, and on the west side of Grand Avenue, the building is now a five-unit apartment house known as the Gallery. (Courtesy of Dr. Lynn A. Partry.)

On the northwest corner of Grand and Sewell Avenues, the second World War II–era USO club was replaced by a modern brick hall built by American Legion Post 24. The post bought the USO property at a city tax sale in 1946 for $1,500. (Author's collection.)

As with many organizations based in Asbury Park, members came from the city's growing post–World War II suburbs. The women in this Legion auxiliary group were grandmothers, daughters, sisters, aunts, the wives of men who served our country, and women who may have enlisted themselves. (Author's collection.)

As post membership dwindled in the early 1980s, Asbury Park High School alumna Esther Piekarski Lysaght, class of 1972, worked out an arrangement to start an innovative preschool program in the American Legion building, while letting the remaining members continue to meet. The school serves children three to five years old and offers a summer camp for all Monmouth County residents ages three to seven. In 2019, Alphabets Preschool Center celebrated its 37th anniversary. (Author's collection.)

Cramped and outmoded, the 1885 Bond Street School property occupied just half the block between Summerfield and Monroe Avenues. Deferred maintenance hastened the antiquated building's end. Demolished in 1993, a modern pre-Kindergarten to fifth-grade elementary school and campus designed for the entire block from Bond to Emory Streets replaced it. It was named for the first African American justice appointed to the US Supreme Court, Thurgood Marshall. (Author's collection.)

Heading east on Cookman Avenue from Grand Avenue, visitors once encountered an entertainment intersection at Summerfield Avenue. On the north side was the Shore Grill, a quiet watering hole with a piano bar bought by Maggie Hogan, who turned it into Chez-L, a popular lesbian gathering spot. Next door, song-and-dance man Eddie King had a studio. It later became the Odyssey nightclub, where Eartha Kitt once performed. Its next incarnation was as Club Phoenix, which closed long before demolition in 2012. (Author's collection.)

The Summerfield extension was renamed to honor city councilman, jazz buff, and nightclub owner Bill Green, who tried different names for the venue that was Fox's Tavern during World War II, including Rustic Lodge, Countrypolitan, and finally the Plantation Room, where many went to hear bebop jazz guitarist Tal Farlow perform. The building was part of the 300 block of Cookman Avenue's south side. (Author's collection.)

Built by I.R. Taylor, the triangular building that would later be occupied by the Plantation Room was the original location of commercial photographer Frank H. Cole, the first authorized Eastman Kodak dealer in New Jersey in 1901. Cole moved his business to Bangs Avenue to be closer to the post office. His extensive mail order printing and developing business is said to have led to an increase in the post office's size. The Jersey City native was a veteran of the Spanish-American War and World War I and was active in the campaign for a city manager form of government in Asbury Park. He died in 1952 at the age of 78. (Author's collection.)

Heading north from Ocean Grove across Wesley Lake on the Heck Street bridge led to the Rollo Transit bus terminal on the left and a cab company on the right. The four-story building in the left background was the second clubhouse for Elks Lodge 128. In the 1940s, it was purchased by the Charms Candy Company for use as a packing plant. Its last hurrah was as the gay disco M&K. It was torn down in December 2009. (Author's collection.)

The 300 and 400 blocks of Cookman Avenue were bisected by Monroe Avenue. Seen in this c. 1940 photograph is the sign on the west wall of Walter Reade's Mayfair Theatre, which fronted on St. James Place. Among the Cookman businesses were Paddy's Bar, run by Patrick Ryan from 1938 to 1973, and a steakhouse operated by Harry Kaiserian. The Bryn Mawr Hotel was across the avenue. (Author's collection.)

After the last remaining buildings were razed, Cookman and Lake Avenues and many of their triangular blocks were reconfigured. In 2006, Kushner Companies of Florham Park built Wesley Gove. Its Westminster Management division handled the marketing of the 91 apartments, duplex, and triplex condos that make up the residences (left) seen here from Asbury Avenue. The 34-unit Monroe Asbury Park (right), apartments built by iStar Inc. of New York, were erected in 2016 on the former Elks/Charms building site. (Author's collection.)

A frozen Wesley Lake, seen here around 1960, offers a rare winter view along with a skyline that once produced magic and civic awe. From right to left are the Palace merry-go-round and Ferris wheel, followed by its 1950s modern addition; the Mayfair Theatre, designed by Thomas Lamb; the second JCP&L building, followed by its first building at 601 Bangs Avenue; and finally, Steinbach's Department Store, recognized by its clock tower. (Author's collection.)

This 1959 view of the amusement circuit's southern loop is from the roof of the Casino carousel house. The former Plaza Hotel site was used for parking. The sprawling West End Hotel succumbed to a mysterious fire in the early 1960s and was replaced by the 220-unit Philips Seaview, a high-rise for low-income residents. The Flamingo Motel was built fronting Kingsley Street. It was demolished to make way for VIVE, a 28-unit condominium built by iStar in 2013. (Author's collection.)

In 1986, George A. Lange and Jules Resnick sold the Palace Amusements complex between Cookman and Lake Avenues and Kingsley Street to developer Henry Vaccaro. Looking for a different kind of attraction than kiddie rides for another ambitious redevelopment plan, he offered 900 square feet to Billy Smith and Steve Bumball, two serious memorabilia collectors who created the Asbury Park Rock 'N' Roll Museum, a first anywhere on the Jersey Shore, in 1987. (Author's collection.)

Also a first for Asbury Park, the museum brought in music fans from all over as well as celebrities—the kind of attention the city used to enjoy. The highlight for Steve Bumball (left) and Billy Smith (right) was the night Bruce Springsteen came inside for a private tour in 1987. He was shooting a music video for *Tunnel of Love* across Kingsley Street in the Casino. Patiently waiting outside the glass doors was a photographer at the start of her career. (Courtesy of Debra L. Rothenberg Photography.)

To fulfill a clause in his contract for the waterfront redevelopment (see chapter two) with Connecticut developer Joseph F. Carabetta, Henry Vaccaro sold the Palace to Carabetta in 1989. But the building's potential was still viable when Springsteen fans from Washington, DC—Deborah Robinson and Bob Crane—launched a public dialogue to repurpose the complex for mixed-use residential lofts and gallery space. (Author's collection.)

In the end, the Save Tillie campaign became an all-out effort to salvage the cultural artifacts that made the property unique to Asbury Park. More in-depth information can be found at savetillie.com. In May 2004, the entertainment buildings that included the Lyric Theatre-turned-adult-film-house ParkCinema, plus the late-night eatery the Talking Bird and Anybody's Café, were torn down and the streets reconfigured. (Author's collection.)

During the height of World War II, the Hurricane of 1944 devastated boardwalk businesses along New Jersey's coast. Years of deferred maintenance turned the boards into veritable matchsticks tossed against the brick arcades. Seen here are the concessions that catered to African Americans who were segregated to the beach south of the Casino since its construction in 1929. The building fronted the heating plant. Deep under the sand ran a pipe that discharged stormwater and other roadway runoff into the sea from further up Wesley Lake and Springwood Avenue. (Author's collection.)

By the time this photograph of the Casino arena was taken in 1998, the Big Band era, ice skating and circus acts, and traveling rock shows such as Hot Tuna were fading into memories. Breaking into the sagging building designed by New York architect Whitney Warren became a rite of passage for many who nicknamed it "the arboretum" for all the vegetation growing freely inside. (Author's collection.)

Greek immigrants Peter and Sophia Heleotis opened the Mayfair grill inside the Casino in 1952, linking its name to the famous theater just two blocks away. In the next generation, Ted and Diane Heleotis kept the eatery going through the bleak years along the boardwalk (seen here in 2002), serving classic Jersey Shore staples like hamburgers with pork roll and funnel cake. In 2010, Diane and her son Jason moved the Mayfair into a modern pop-up container provided by Madison Marquette at Third Avenue. (Author's collection.)

For 20 years, the lot at the corner of Ocean and Asbury Avenues stood empty. In a 1954 tax sale for $85,000, the city sold half the block to David Cronheim of Newark, with a stipulation that he improve the lot with a seven-story elevator building. The resulting Empress Motel fell on hard times late in the 20th century. In 1998, Shep Pettibone bought it. In 1999, he opened Paradise, a nightclub catering to the new wave of gay and lesbian visitors. In 2004, he reopened the four-story 101-room motel as the upscale Empress Hotel. In the background is the notorious Gold Digger Bar and C-8, the failed high-rise. (Author's collection.)

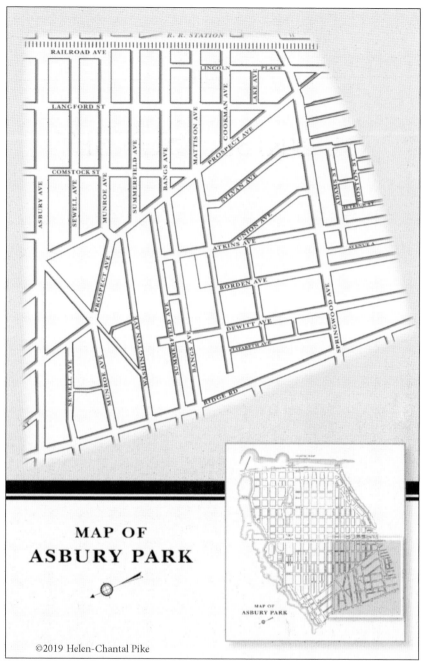

MAP OF ASBURY PARK

MAP OF
ASBURY PARK

This chapter is divided into two sections. The first half covers the northeast neighborhood, from Sunset Avenue to Deal Lake and west to Main Street. The second half begins on page 64 and covers locations south of Fifth Avenue to First Avenue and west to the 800 block at Main Street. A lot of early history was covered in Images of America: *Asbury Park*, published in 1997. A closer look at the competition between the city-owned oceanfront and private businesses can be found in *Asbury Park's Glory Days: The Story of an American Resort*, published in 2005. This chapter, like the rest of this book, gives some context to events and addresses, especially ones that emerged after 1980. (Map by author.)

Two

SUNRISE, SUNSET

Founder James A. Bradley's death on June 6, 1921, in Manhattan signaled the end of the 1890s City Beautiful movement in Asbury Park. Led by architects, landscapers, and reformers, including Protestant ministers, the urban-planning crusade was designed to create orderly cities with parks to make urban areas more livable. When city leaders posthumously put up the Bradley statue by Giuseppe Moretti, the founder could symbolically look out on the ocean from Atlantic Square. It anchored the park designed for Sunset Lake. Bradley's unobstructed view of the sea did not last, however. Mayor Clarence E.F. Hetrick's ambition to have a convention hall (ConHall) and theater complex to compete with Atlantic City ushered in a completely different era in city affairs. (Author's collection.)

The debate over private versus public ownership and management of the boardwalk started when Bradley was pressured to turn over the oceanfront to the city along with the sewer system. It was not until 2007, and a series of successive property sales and management contracts, that ConHall's interior storefronts were filled year-round due to the efforts of the Washington, DC–based real estate services firm Madison Marquette. The company turned the complex into a year-round shopping and entertainment destination that includes a spectacularly lit Christmas tree for the holiday season. (Photograph by Chris Spiegel, courtesy of Madison Marquette.)

The ShoreCats, a US Basketball League team (1998–2000), was owned by the New Jersey Hoop Group: George Michals (whose family had owned a seafood restaurant on Ocean at Second), lawyer Tony Caruso, and sports mogul Jim Jennings. This pregame event on April 28, 2000, recognized a number of civic groups and individuals, including musician Heshy "The Hesh" Rosenwasser, the author, and Kerry Butch, executive director of the short-lived Asbury Park Consortium, a coalition that provided much-needed training in civic engagement. (Author's collection.)

Industry veteran Diane Raver established the Garden State Film Festival in 2002, tapping a wealth of established New Jersey–based talent to participate in an annual spring convention for aspiring filmmakers, screenwriters, and actors of all ages. It was the first successful initiative that took Asbury Park beyond just a destination to watch movies. Here, in 2007, she is with actor James Gandolfini from the HBO series *The Sopranos*, in which a number of notable scenes were filmed in Asbury Park. (Courtesy of Diane Raver.)

In 2008, Jason Meehan founded the Zombie Walk, an annual cultural celebration in tune with the city's diverse artistic vibe. It twice made the Guinness Book of World Records: in 2010 with 4,093 zombies, and in 2013 with 9,592 zombies. In 2019, developer and restaurateur John McGuillion, owner of Kim Marie's Eat n Drink Away on Kingsley Street between Sunset and Sixth Avenues, sponsored the event that occurs the first weekend in October. (Photograph by Pasqualina DeBoer, courtesy of Madison Marquette.)

L'ILLUSTRATION

L'INCENDIE TRAGIQUE DU « MORRO CASTLE »: LE PAQUEBOT, ENCORE FUMANT, ÉCHOUÉ DEVANT LA PLAGE D'ASBURY PARK.
DANS LE NEW JERSEY

AVEC CE NUMÉRO L'ABONNEMENT N° I COMPREND "LA PETITE ILLUSTRATION" CONTENANT

AVANT L'OUBLI (Ecrire)

(En trois parties. — III.)

Souvenirs d'HENRI LAVEDAN, de l'Académie française.

13, RUE SAINT-GEORGES, PARIS (9°)   Voir au verso les tarifs d'abonnement.

In 2009, the Asbury Park Historical Society erected the first known commemorative monument to the doomed ocean liner *Morro Castle* on the 75th anniversary of the tragic accident that claimed the lives of 137 passengers. The burning ship had beached within a stone's throw of ConHall. After Madison Marquette took control of the boardwalk, it saw an opportunity to create a landscaped public square for other monuments relating to Asbury Park's history along with a much wider access to the boardwalk from Ocean Avenue at Fifth Avenue. (Author's collection.)

The memorial garden includes the bust of Greek Archbishop Athenagoras of North and South America, who initiated an annual blessing of the ocean. It was erected in 1975, three years after his death. The third monument is the plaque donated in 2006 by musician and record producer Doc Holiday ("Fast Eddie" Wohanka) to honor the founding musicians of the Sound of Asbury Park (SOAP) around 1960. A second plaque was added in 2008. (Courtesy of Gary Crawford.)

Now called the Berkeley Oceanfront Hotel and managed by Amsterdam Hospitality of New York, the Berkeley-Carteret Hotel was built by Arthur C. Steinbach and his investors after quietly negotiating with the Bradley estate to buy the block. Steinbach hired Whitney Warren, also of New York, to design a cross-shaped hotel that opened in 1925. Warren was subsequently hired by the city to design the Paramount Theatre–Convention Hall complex, plus a matching redbrick Sunset Avenue pavilion, with a pedestrian bridge connecting it to the hotel. (Author's collection.)

Dr. Sebastian and Rosemarie Vaccaro pose with guests at their wedding reception in 1934 in the Crystal Ballroom of the Berkeley-Carteret Hotel. Dr. Vaccaro was the son of Italian immigrants who had settled on the west side. After earning a medical degree from Georgetown University, he returned to Asbury Park, married Rosemarie, a registered nurse, and in 1939 opened a practice at 509 Fourth Avenue, where the couple raised a family. With office hours seven days a week, Dr. Vaccaro also made house calls, often to patients who were themselves descendants of immigrants, plus the growing African American population who lived in his childhood neighborhood. In 1983, his sons Henry and Sam, along with business partners, bought the long-neglected hotel and launched an ambitious $16 million effort to make it the jewel in the crown for Asbury Park's oceanfront comeback. They reopened it in 1985 to rave reviews. Henry Vaccaro recounts this period in the city's history in his memoir *Johnny Cash is a Friend of Mine*, published in 2013. It includes a perspective on the nation's savings and loan crisis of the 1980s and 1990s, during which the brothers lost over 25 properties in the beachfront development zone alone and went into bankruptcy. (Courtesy of Henry Vaccaro Sr.)

In 1987, the Vaccaro brothers teamed up with another descendant of Italian immigrants from the West Side, Hollywood actor Danny DeVito. DeVito made the hotel the site of the world premiere of his directorial debut, *Throw Momma From The Train*, the cult classic he wrote and also starred in with Billy Crystal. (Courtesy of Joan Flatley.)

Torn down in 1963, the former Monterey Hotel block north of the Berkeley, between Sixth and Seventh Avenues, was developed into a three-building condo complex with Spanish names: Seville, Monterey, and Barcelona (seen here). Better known as North Beach, the complex was designed by SOSH Architects of Atlantic City for Paramount Homes; the first unit sold in 2008. (Courtesy of Steve Albert.)

Second-generation resident Gary Giberson, left, began working for the city in his teens as a locker boy and retired as public works director in 2014. He is seen here in 1998 with another lifelong resident, beachfront director Joe Pallotto, when that office was in the Fifth Avenue Pavilion. Pallotto has also served as president of the Asbury Park Fishing Club, the oldest saltwater fishing club in the United States, started in 1888 by James Bradley. (Author's collection.)

From a humble, wood-frame building for the Asbury Park Fishing Club donated by Bradley to the expanded Marine Grill lost to fire, the highly prized site between Deal Lake and the ocean remains the city's last open expanse—though not from lack of trying to have it generate revenue. In 1964, the city hoped for a 20-story apartment house with 11 stores and a restaurant. In 1966, it was a 10-story Holiday Inn. In 2019, it is still a public beach. (Author's collection.)

One of 300 Asbury Park hotels in 1908 was the St. Laurent Hotel on Seventh Avenue, between Park and Grand Avenues. New owners in 1941 changed the name to Tides Hotel. In the 21st century renaissance, the property was bought by Martin Santomenno, who, with his partner Joseph Rufino and two family members, spent three years and an estimated $2 million to bring an Art Deco luster to the venerable property, along with a French restaurant, an outdoor pool lounge, and a gallery-performance space in the intimate lobby. (Author's collection.)

The daughter of Rev. Howard T. Widdemer of the First Congregational Church, poet-novelist Margaret Widdemer, was living here on the southwest corner of Seventh and Grand Avenues in 1918 when she tied with Carl Sandburg for the Pulitzer Prize for her collection of poetry *The Old Road to Paradise*. With greater Asbury Park to inspire her fiction, she penned at least four young-adult novels. She died in 1978 in Gloversville, New York. (Author's collection.)

This rare postcard shows the bright yellow paint that made the Burns Bradshaw real estate agency hard to miss. It still retains its Dutch-gambrel cottage character on the east side of Main Street between Seventh and Sixth Avenues. Marty Bradshaw continues the business she once shared with the late Georgia Pappyliou Burns, whose immigrant family had a boardwalk concession in the 1930s. (Author's collection.)

Modest single-family homes on Main Street's east side between Sixth and Sunset Avenues were cleared in the 1930s for this 22-unit residential complex with storefronts on the sidewalk level. The add-on had been a combination hobby and bicycle store. Empty in this photograph, it waits for a new tenant. In 1960, that would be the deli opened by Frank P.J. Maggio, a World War II veteran and a junior partner in Baldanza's Bakery in Long Branch. (Author's collection.)

Maura Maggio Marrucca, holding one of the hundreds of loaves baked daily, and her brother Joe are the third generation in the city's food industry, operating their late father's landmark deli on Main Street between Sixth and Sunset Avenues. Their grandfather, Tom Maggio, had operated C. Maggio Groceries in Asbury Park in the 1920s. (Author's collection.)

This was the aftermath of the 1957 fire that claimed the Columbia Hotel built by W. Harvey Jones, who took ownership of Buchanan & Smock Lumber in 1925. The fire also destroyed the Hotel Commodore next door, a rooming house, and a garage. The lots remained vacant for decades but came in handy for parking on busy holiday weekends and during big events. (Photograph by Milton Edelman, author's collection.)

The rest of this chapter features various locations and their stories from Fifth Avenue south to First Avenue and west to Main Street. This 1998 aerial view shows the oceanfront 10 years after the much-hoped-for condo development stalled due to the banking and real estate market collapse of the early 1990s—an economic pattern that would repeat again in the new century. The city had awarded a waterfront redevelopment contract to the partnership of Henry and Sam Vaccaro and Joseph Carabetta of Meriden, Connecticut. But when the financial and property markets took a beating and banks stopped their loans, the city's redevelopment rights got mired in nine years of bankruptcy proceedings in Connecticut. In 2002, the *Wall Street Journal* reported that Ocean Front Acquisitions purchased the development rights for $7.4 million and paid Asbury Park $6.5 million in back taxes. A principal in Ocean Front Acquisitions was Larry Fishman. From September 2001 to February 2009, he was the chief operating officer of Asbury Partners. (Courtesy of Kathy Dorn Severini.)

When the outlook was much rosier, Joe Carabetta made a donation to the chamber of commerce in 1992, then running on a shoestring in a building near the bend of Asbury and Ocean Avenues it shared with the city's beach department. Accepting the donation is Executive Director Joan McLaughlin Flatley. (Courtesy of Joan Flatley.)

Asbury Partners pledged an infrastructure upgrade of the storm sewer system and sewer lines, plus a rehab of ConHall and the Casino and attached heating plant, along with rebuilding the boardwalk, as seen here. (Author's collection.)

Veteran journalists and music fans Jean Mickle and Stan Goldstein teamed up to offer music heritage tours for foreign fans who wanted to trace Bruce Springsteen's early career influences. Their first tour was in 1999. Not much was open, yet music tourists kept coming. By 2002, when this photograph was taken in the Paramount lobby during an antique appraisal fair, the pair had a well-researched companion book. The fourth edition of *Rock & Roll Tour of the Jersey Shore* was published in 2014. (Author's collection.)

On the southwest corner of Fifth and Ocean Avenues, musician Lance Larson and his longtime partner Debbie DeLisa opened Lance & Debbie's in 2002. They did not have a liquor license, so they hosted dance parties. Soon, the former name, Wonder Bar, was added to the marquee along with a liquor license and a business partner, Pat Schiavino, who struck a deal for a 50th-anniversary Corvette photoshoot, which included getting most of the venue painted in the iconic 1950s color and motifs of Palace Amusements. (Author's collection.)

The Wonder Bar caters equally to music and sports fans, but most belovedly to dogs and their owners with a fair-weather "Yappy Hour" on the bar's south side. Debbie DeLisa is also the executive director of Asbury Boardwalk Rescue, a nonprofit dedicated to the care of cats and other neglected animals in the city. (Photograph by Victor Bubadias, courtesy of Madison Marquette.)

Owned by iStar, the lender-turned-developer that bought the former Salvation Army retirement home, The Asbury opened in 2016 and is managed as a Salt Hotel. Partners David Bowd and Kevin O'Shea gave the boxy building a retro-fresh makeover that included a large portrait of Bishop Francis Asbury in the new atrium lobby and placement of Walter Reade's Baronet Theatre sign on an exterior wall used for showing second-run movies in the summer. (Author's collection.)

During stretches when he was working on new material, Bruce Springsteen could be seen live in unannounced appearances, such as this 30-minute set during the Clearwater Festival in Sunset Park in 2001. Originally held at Sandy Hook, Clearwater was founded by musician Bob Killian, whom activist and folk musician Peter Seeger mentored. Seeger pioneered the clean water movement in 1966. In 2006, Springsteen released *We Shall Overcome: The Seeger Sessions*. (Courtesy of Ellen Carroll.)

Patrick and Sandy (Beatrice) Breslin's enormous generosity shown to the military stationed at Fort Monmouth, Camp Evans, Earle Naval Weapons Station, and even Fort Dix during World War II and the Korean Conflict earned them accolades and, ultimately, this commemorative stone in Sunset Lake Memorial Park. Also known as Veterans Park, it is on the south side of Sunset Lake between Bergh and Heck Streets and features other granite markers for individuals and groups that deserve to be remembered. (Author's collection.)

On December 7, 1941, when Japan attacked Pearl Harbor, the Breslins (right) moved from Camden in South Jersey to Monmouth County to open a tackle, bait, fishing boat, and food concession on the Shark River. This stone near Pat and Sandy's Pier in the Belmar Yacht Basin was their public thank-you to the US armed forces. The Breslins lived on Bergh Street. In the last seven years of their lives together, they ran a rooming house, most likely in the 300 block of Sewell Avenue. Sandy, who had been born in Ireland, died in 1963 at age 63. (Photograph by Milton Edelman, author's collection.)

Sunset Park's west end is fronted by Main Street. Crossing its Fifth Avenue corner in this photograph, a pedestrian appears headed to the Acme grocery store on the southwest corner whose c. 1930s sign covers part of the uniquely patterned brick building that once held the Pennypacker Press. Operated by three brothers from Philadelphia, it printed souvenir booklets and the *Asbury Park Journal*. (Author's collection.)

In 1901, the Pennypackers filled in the alley between their building and the one next door on Fifth Avenue, creating a building so narrow—10 feet wide—that the apartment house made an appearance in *Ripley's Believe It or Not.* (Courtesy of Steve Albert.)

The Fifth Avenue Tavern was a frequent stop for an end-of-shift pint by workers at Fischer's Bakery, right around the corner on Railroad Avenue. But when Fischer's closed, the tavern fell on hard times. In 1999, George Lister bought the property and renamed it Georgie's, establishing an atmosphere that has earned it the reputation as "the gay Cheers." (Courtesy of Lisa Carlson.)

Visible from the alley that runs along Georgie's is all that is left of the North Asbury Drugstore. When the store next to "the world's skinniest apartment house" was sold, its classic soda fountain that was popular with high school students was shipped out of state. (Courtesy of Steve Albert.)

South of Pennypackers' printing plant on Main Street was the Cameo Bar, which earned its name from the mannequin busts embedded in the barback thanks to a patron working off a tab who was employed in creative services at Steinbach Department Store. Seen here in 1997 are longtime friends and barkeeps Betty Petillo (left) and Irene Wilson, whose late husband, Palmy, left her the bar. (Author's collection.)

Radically repainted a midnight blue from its original white, Madame Marie's fortune-telling booth is still on the boardwalk at Fourth Avenue. Behind it, and occupying the entire block between Fourth and Third Avenues, the new 17-story Asbury Ocean Club designed by Handel Architects of New York is the second tallest high-rise overlooking the ocean after Asbury Tower, at 24 floors. Owned by developer iStar, the club is part of a $300 million, 35-acre portfolio whose 35-room hotel is managed as a Salt Hotel while 130 units are residences. It was finished in 2019. (Author's collection.)

The Jefferson Hotel was on the southeast corner of Fourth Avenue and Kingsley Street. Its bar featured a jukebox, a bartender who doubled as a bookie, and a barback painting of dancing dogs. The after-hours saloon that served at least until 5:00 a.m. became known in the 1970s and early 1980s as a hangout for musicians such as Southside Johnny and the Asbury Jukes and Bruce Springsteen. The hotel came down in the late 1980s in anticipation of an oceanfront renaissance. (Author's collection.)

Lolita Lip and the Lipman (Joan and Mark Lipman) had an original comedy-rock ensemble with songs such as "You Smell Like Lox and I Love You." In the 1980s, the former deputy clerk and her engineer husband were frequent entertainers at Pancho Villa's on the northwest corner of Fourth Avenue and Kingsley Street in the former Finaldi's Italian restaurant. The Mexican restaurant's last name before it closed was Taxco Village. (Courtesy of Joan Lipman.)

Originally built as a garage for an apartment building, the Fastlane, with its stadium seating, had several name changes along with openings and closings before it was torn down in 2013. Nonetheless, it was a musician's proving ground, including for the frontman of Atlantic City Expressway, a high school senior from Sayreville by the name of John Bongiovi. (Author's collection.)

Between the Fastlane and Asbury Lanes, the 1913 Ocean Theatre was bought by theater mogul Walter Reade Jr. in 1953. Repurposing the marquee from one of his Manhattan theaters in 1962, he renamed it the Baronet. The Art Deco jewel featured a stage with a proscenium arch. Despite various attempts to put the property back into commercial use, it was closed in 2007. The roof caved in during the winter of 2009, and it was torn down in 2010. (Author's collection.)

In 2004, Asbury Lanes owner Ralph Ayles brought in promoter Mel Stultz, who had the short-lived bar Odd Fellows Lodge at 660 Cookman Avenue, to transform the staid bowling alley and cocktail lounge into an edgy performance venue. Jenn Hampton, co-owner of the Parlor Gallery on Cookman, took over management and bookings, along with Laney Switzer. They brought in film actor Crispin Glover (pictured), cult film director John Waters, saucy burlesque dancers the Pontani Sisters, and goth acts, among others. A dropdown screen doubled for vintage horror flicks. After a succession of property sales, iStar bought the Lanes in 2015 and closed it for renovations. It reopened in 2018. (Photograph by Mike McLaughlin, courtesy of Jenn Hampton.)

Multidisciplinary artist Michael LaValle, who studied at the University of the Arts in Philadelphia, is best known by his artistic alias, Porkchop, and his public murals, including this early one painted on the east side exterior wall of Asbury Lanes and seen from Kingsley after the Baronet Theater and the Fastlane were demolished. (Courtesy of Steve Albert.)

As Fourth Avenue continues west, its original single-family residential character starts to reemerge, especially after Heck Street. At No. 509, on the north side of the street, a young Henry Vaccaro, dressed smartly in military uniform, and his sister Frances strike a pose outside the house that doubled as the medical office of their father, Dr. Sebastian Vaccaro. This photograph was taken in the early 1940s, before their two siblings were born. (Courtesy of Henry V. Vaccaro.)

The Asbury Park Historical Society board of trustees for 2019–2020 is pictured here. From left to right are photographer-businesswoman Kay Harris, incoming president; Teddy Chomko, fundraising; Andy Skokos, vice president–treasurer; Jim Henry, vice president–legal affairs; Susan Rosenberg, secretary; Don Stine, outgoing president; Mary D'Amato, treasurer; Frank D'Alessandro, retired high school math teacher and property owner who donated Arbutus Cottage to the society in 2015; artist Dolly Sternesky, grants; and Councilwoman Eileen Chapman, special events. Not pictured is Jennifer Stine, in charge of web and social media. Susan C. Skokos, who took the photograph, filled the slot vacated by D'Alessandro, who stepped down at the end of 2019. Incoming president Kay Harris represents the third generation of her family to serve on the board. Outgoing president Don Stine's tenure included the installation of the black granite *Morro Castle* monument in front of the Paramount Theater, restoration of the famous Rainbow Room and Turf Club neon nightclub signs and their placement in public places, and the listing of Arbutus Cottage (Crane House) on both the state (2014) and national (2015) historic registers. Built in 1878 as a private residence, Asbury Park's first permanent museum is west of Grand Avenue, on the south side of the street at 508 Fourth Avenue. (Courtesy of the Asbury Park Historical Society.)

The only home still standing in New Jersey where journalist and author Stephen Crane once lived, the property is also a repository of artifacts from buildings that gave Asbury Park its unique history, including the Mayfair Theater's lobby fountain, saved from the wrecking ball in 1974 by Peter Palumbo, who had it moved to his home on Sunset Avenue. It is also where one can find the museum's program director, writer-in-residence, and society trustee Tom Chesek, who penned *Legendary Locals of Asbury Park*, published in 2015. (Author's collection.)

In 2002, Carol and David Gilliland (left) and Malcolm Navias (third from left), converted a car dealership on the northwest corner of Fourth Avenue and Main Street into an antiques emporium named for the automobile once sold there: Studebaker's. They are joined here for the ribbon-cutting ceremony by, from left to right, council representatives Kate Mellina and John Lofreddo, Fr. Robert F. Kaeding, and Navias's partner Tom Pivinski. (Courtesy of Malcolm Navias.)

Since 2009, collector extraordinaire Robert Ilvento has anchored the northern spot of the Third Avenue Arcade with his wildly successful Silverball Pinball Museum. For many who recall the 1950s boardwalk games of skill, this interactive museum is the closest one can come to going home. The museum's website says it best: "a living, breathing and blinking tribute to our pinball and video gaming past." (Photograph by Allison Nugent, courtesy of Madison Marquette.)

West on Third Avenue to the southeast corner of Grand Avenue was the 1905 home of Dr. James F. Ackerman—the first to break with the residential resort's 19th-century Victorian aesthetic. Across Grand and on the next block south, Dr. Ackerman saw patients (see chapter one). In 1931, Ackerman, who helmed the Ann May Hospital in Spring Lake, was made president of the Fitkin-Morgan Memorial Hospital in Neptune. He died in 1934. The house was torn down sometime after 1970. (Courtesy of Dr. Lynn A. Parry.)

At a 1931 family reunion, Anna Rouse Ackerman (far left) holds her grandson Lynn A. Parry. With her are, from left to right, (first row) grandchildren Joan (Forsythe) and Carol (Parker) Cole, Dottie and Marsha Cole (Doleman); O.K. Parry Jr., and Jimmy Fisher Jr.; (second row) son-in-law Dr. Oliver Kessler Parry, Dr. Ackerman, daughter Dorothy and husband architect Frank Cole, daughter Janet and husband Dr. James Fisher, and daughter Carol A. Parry. In the left window is Ann Parry (Gosling). Both she and Lynn A. Parry later became doctors. (Courtesy of Dr. Lynn A. Parry.)

Farther west on Third Avenue is the Center and Center House, meeting the needs of those living with HIV/AIDS. From a storefront on Mattison Avenue in the Kinmonth Building in 1992 to the renovated residential property that opened in 2006 at 806 Third Avenue (site of former Tilton's Clover Leaf Dairy Bar), the Center has been the vision of Fr. Bob Kaeding, a progressive Catholic priest who was pastor of St. Anslem's in Wayside for 21 years. Originally from North Plainfield and ordained in 1973, Father Bob retired in 2019. (Courtesy of the Center.)

With the city as her culinary canvas, restaurant mogul, philanthropist, activist, and wonderfully inventive Marilyn Schlossbach opened Langosta Lounge in November 2008, followed by Pop's Garage, Lighted Salted, and the Asbury Park Yacht Club. At the same time, she had a ground-breaking deli and cafe on Cookman Avenue designed for the CBD's emerging residential population, Market in the Middle. On July 14, 2006, she married Scott Szegeski there. (Courtesy of Marilyn Schlossbach.)

The immensely talented blues-rock guitarist G.E. Smith, former leader of the Saturday Night Live Band and lead guitarist for Philadelphia's Hall & Oates, headlined the Stone Pony, playing with R&B musician Southside Johnny Lyon. Smith's appearance was part of a long tradition of national names and enthusiastic audiences at the legendary club. (Courtesy of Dave Christopher.)

GRAND OPENING

FRIDAY, 25 SEPTEMBER- resident DJ Aqua presents renown DJ, producer
and remixer

Johnny Vicious

SATURDAY, 26 SEPTEMBER - *Vinyl* presents DJ UNIQUE and
Tommy Boy Records recording artist

Amber

serving cocktails 'til 2am, music 'til 6am
doors at 9pm • 21 and over, please
3,000 square feet of underground bliss
champagne VIP lounge • outdoor bar
reduced admission with card
dress like you mean it

Vinyl

Second and Ocean Ave.
Asbuy Park, NJ USA
e-mail for info: DJAquaUSA@aol.com

Original Stone Pony owners Jack Roig and Butch Pielka closed the club in 1991. Steve and Judy Nasar briefly tried a dance club, Vinyl, but closed it in 1998. (Author's collection.)

In 2000, Jersey City restaurateur Domenic Santana (center) and partners bought the 1920s eatery-turned-nightclub for $375,000 and reopened the Pony over Memorial Day weekend. In 2003, they sold it to Asbury Partners. It is now managed by Madison Marquette. (Author's collection.)

In 1962, the cast-iron lampposts from the 19th-century West End Hotel on Asbury Avenue at Kingsley Street were reinstalled in front of the library on First Avenue at Grand Avenue when the hotel was torn down to be replaced by Philips Seaview. In 2011, an out-of-control car damaged one post. It took five years to get two near-duplicate posts to grace the main entrance again, while the remaining original lamppost was relocated to the children's library entrance on Grand. The ADA-compliant handicap ramp on Grand was made possible by a generous donation from Bruce Springsteen and was built to coincide with the Smithsonian Institution's traveling music exhibit in 2012. (Author's collection.)

In 2010, the New Jersey History listserv featured a request for proposals to host *New Harmonies: Celebrating American Roots Music*. Involving the city's economic development director Tom Gilmour resulted in the winning bid. The Asbury Park: Where Music Lives committee, which included the author (left), tapped the library to host the exhibit, which drew residents who had moved away, such as photographer-author Madonna Carter Jackson and her mother, Lenora Niblack Carter, daughter and widow, respectively, of noted West Side photographer Joseph A. Carter Sr. (Author's collection.)

Despite the presence of corporate chains, Home Drug Store on the southeast corner of First Avenue and Main Street since at least the 1950s remains resolutely independently owned, with pharmacist Vishal "Vic" Sood buying the business in 2007. (Courtesy of Steve Albert.)

The Napolitano family sponsored Aniello "Danny" De Sena's passage from Saviano, Italy, outside Naples; he arrived in 1923 at age 23 with $1.35 in his pocket. In the days before electricity and refrigeration were widespread, he opened Danny's Ice & Fuel at 810 First Avenue. When gas heat became prevalent, the next generation closed the doors in Asbury Park. However, his grandson Danny resumed the family business as Midway Gas & Fuel. The family name can be found spelled de Sena, De Seno, and DeSeno. (Author's collection.)

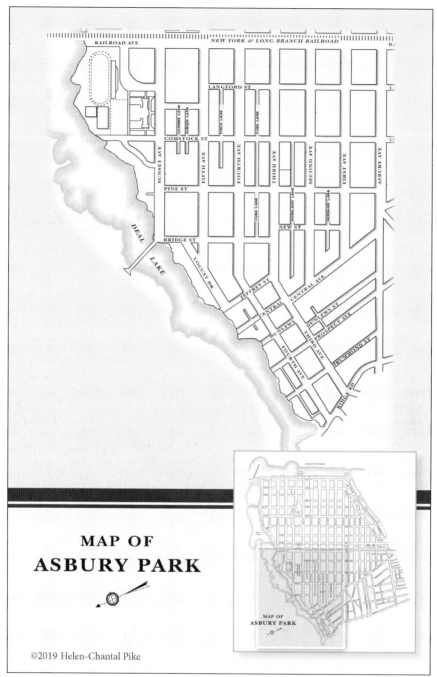

MAP OF
ASBURY PARK

MAP OF
ASBURY PARK

©2019 Helen-Chantal Pike

Springwood Avenue was the city's first west-east boulevard to be laid out in the 19th century. It linked the ocean to the rise of land known locally as Sand Hill in the section of West Park (present-day Neptune). The inhabitants were the Richardson and Revey families who became known as Sand Hill Indians and were part of the Lenape and Cherokee Tribe. Skilled at carpentry, some of their descendants worked for James A. Bradley in the 1870s, building numerous structures in Asbury Park. For a deeper understanding of the area's Native American presence, please visit the nonprofit sandhillindianhistory.com. (Map by author.)

84

Three

BLACK AND BLUE

Nowhere was Asbury Park more ready for the Jazz Age than Springwood Avenue. With *Asbury Park South*, New York painter Florine Stettheimer celebrated the Harlem Renaissance in 1920 while the beach in Asbury Park was segregated. But with a racial and ethnic mix of businesses closer to the highways, Springwood was better positioned to host entertainers for audiences who appreciated cutting-edge music. The 1978 musical revue *Ain't Misbehavin'* was a tribute to this era, featuring songs written by jazz pianist Fats Waller and his lyricist Andy Razaf, who together wrote "Honeysuckle Rose" in a second-story apartment on Atkins Avenue. The revue also included another song by the pair, "Black and Blue"—the high school colors. As with chapter two, this section has two parts. In the first half are stories of a diverse neighborhood between Springwood and Asbury Avenues' south sides, from Railroad Avenue west to Neptune at Ridge Avenue. The second half shows some of the progress made more than two decades after the civil disturbance of 1970. (Courtesy of Michael Rosenfeld Gallery LLC.)

Dolores "Dee" Holland started performing at three. By her teens, she was playing with touring names and local musicians, according to fellow musician Dorian Parreott, who said of her, "She's an exceptional musician . . . can memorize anything . . . can improvise on any melody." Dee jammed regularly with jazz sax player Cliff Johnson and drummer Clarence Pinkney, seen here at the Capitol on the southeast corner of Springwood Avenue and Avenue A. (Courtesy of Dolores Holland and the Asbury Park African-American Music Project Inc.)

Still a man of mystery who was born in Passaic in 1913 and lived in Long Branch while wintering in Florida, Leo Karp loved music and publicity, the latter because it was good for business. It is unknown whether he was passionate about golf, the track, or both, but he made the Turf Club on the southwest corner of Springwood and Atkins Avenues a memorable after-hours nightclub in the post–World War II era. (Photograph by Joseph A. Carter Sr., courtesy of Madonna Carter Jackson.)

By the mid-1920s, Philadelphia stage magician and occultist Julius Zancig could no longer afford a summer rental on Cookman Avenue's east side and moved to Springwood Avenue near Atkins Avenue. (Author's collection.)

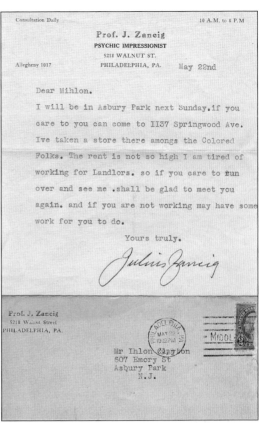

Music historians Pamela and Charles Horner are the guiding force of Classic Urban Harmony LLC, the firm that promotes music through the legacy of rhythm-and-blues vocal group harmony (the 1940s through 1960s), doo-wop, soul harmony, spiritual and gospel quartet singing, and early rock and roll. Their first of a four-volume set, *100 Years of West Side Music*, covers 1871–1945. (Courtesy of Charlie Horner.)

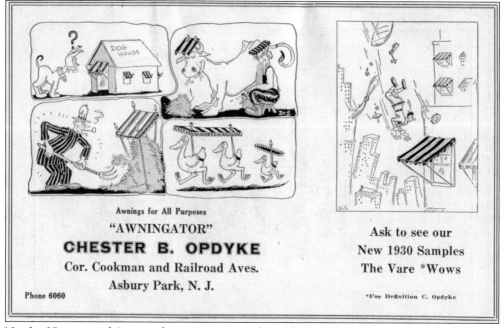

North of Springwood Avenue, the next commercial corridor was Cookman Avenue, where Chester B. Opdyke Sr. launched his awning and canopy business in 1914. Opdyke established a clientele and eventually moved to a larger manufacturing facility in Wall Township and a retail operation in Spring Lake when the intersection with Railroad Avenue was reconfigured. (Author's collection.)

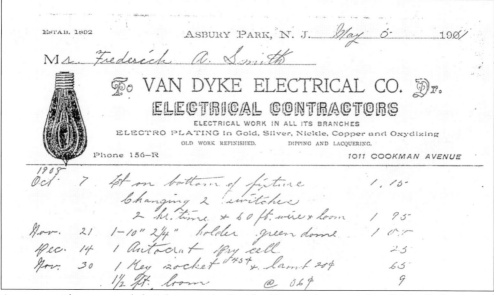

As more residents wanted their homes wired with efficient electricity, Jewell Van Dyke opened a business at 1011 Cookman Avenue west of Langford Street. With the advent of radio, he diversified into retail as an agent for Radiola and Steinite, and promoted his business as "the Home of Reliable Radio." His son Henry, who was hired to string lights across Springwood Avenue for the annual Italian Festival, moved the business west to the expanding suburbs in Neptune. (Author's collection.)

Mount Pisgah Lodge No. 48–Prince Hall Affiliate started to look for a permanent home after sharing quarters on Atkins Avenue with the Reindeer Lodge, a fraternal order that was a breakaway group from the Moose. Originally established in Oakhurst, by 1955, Mount Pisgah bought a property at 930 Cookman Avenue for $15,000 and converted it into a Masonic temple at a cost of $9,000. (Author's collection.)

This building has had quite a history. As a wooden edifice, it began as a Baptist church on Main Street and Bangs Avenue. When James Bradley donated the Cookman Avenue and Langford Street corner to the Sons of Israel, the Orthodox congregation bought the church and relocated it here. At the time, Bethel AME had a masonry house of worship on the southwest corner of Main Street and Second Avenue. The Sons of Israel sold this building to Bethel AME when they moved across Main Street to Asbury and Grand Avenues, where they built a new synagogue on the site of the former Women's Club (which had moved to Allenhurst). Dedicated church members restored it. (Author's collection.)

Police officer James Parreott and his wife, Esther, raised five daughters and two sons at 1022 Mattison Avenue between the 1930s and 1950s. David followed in his father's footsteps while Dorian became a musician, returning as the high school's music director. Their parents' house parties always featured live music and delicious baked foods from his mother. Esther hosted the Almyria Tea Room in their home, catering to summer travelers. (Courtesy of Dorian Parreott.)

Moving from a small house on the northeast corner of Bangs Avenue and Bond Street on the east side to this much larger house on Monroe Avenue on the West Side, the musically talented son of Italian immigrants Louis Miraglia raised a family here while also giving music lessons on the second floor of Cook's Beehive at Cookman Avenue and Main Street. (Author's collection.)

The Monmouth Little Symphony Orchestra

Louis Miraglia, Conductor

Maestro Miraglia also sowed the seeds of the Monmouth Symphony Orchestra. It was launched in 1948 as the Spring Lake Sinfonietta. By 1950, it was known as the Monmouth Little Symphony, seen here performing on the high school's stage. More about all the genres of music and their genesis in this residential resort can be found in *Asbury Park: Where Music Lives*, published in 2011. (Author's collection.)

In the early years, the funeral business was divided among the different faiths. World War I veteran Harry J. Bodine, who doubled as the Monmouth County coroner, handled most of the arrangements for Jewish families. After his passing in 1936, his wife's nephew Richard Hoidal took over the business, eventually moving it to Oakhurst. (Author's collection.)

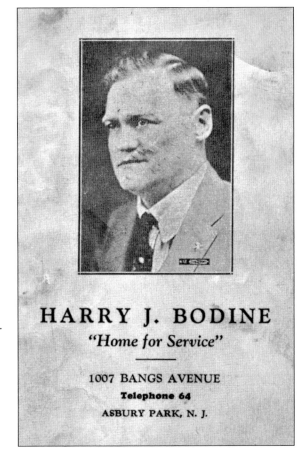

HARRY J. BODINE
"Home for Service"

1007 BANGS AVENUE
Telephone 64
ASBURY PARK, N. J.

At James Bradley's 1921 funeral, the only floral arrangement came from the grateful child welfare home, acknowledging its benefactor who in 1913 donated land on Sewall Avenue and Langford Street plus funds to build a neighborhood clinic. In 1925, it was replaced by a brick masonry building. Today, it houses the Community Affairs & Resource Center, a multilingual, multicultural social service agency for individuals and families whose needs may otherwise go unmet due to language barriers, discrimination, and lack of cultural competency. (Courtesy of Steve Albert.)

JOBS FOR UNEMPLOYED MEN
AND YOUNG MEN WITH APPEARANCE

See FRANK FLEMING, Jr.

1815 Springwood Ave. Near State Highway—AGENT—Phone 4067-W, ASBURY PARK, N. J.

Representing the Largest Tailoring Organization in the United States

THE WOHLMUTH CO. BALTIMORE, MD.

AND

BUY TAILOR MADE CLOTHES

SUITS, OVERCOATS, TOP-COATS $17.50 $22.50 $27.50 $32.50

LATEST STYLES— ANY LENGTH TROUSERS—ANY WIDTH CUFFS AND BOTTOMS

GUARANTEED ALL WOOL   ∾   GUARANTEED TAILORING   ∾   GUARANTEED FIT

The King Press, 8 Sylvan Ave. Asbury Park, N. J.

The King Press at 2 Sylvan Avenue serviced the printing needs of west-side businesses, including this recruitment poster for a business farther west on Springwood Avenue in neighboring Neptune. (Author's collection.)

Noted artist and businessman Lorenzo Harris Sr. (seated), who each year had a mercantile license to build sand sculptures at the First Avenue beach, in 1945 ran for a seat on the city commission under the banner of the West Side Citizens League. It was a bold effort to address growing economic and educational discrimination. He lost. With him in this photograph is his wife, Kathryn, who helped him form the local chapter of the NAACP. He passed away in 1946. (Author's collection.)

Built as a segregated facility in 1913, with smaller classrooms for black pupils, the Bangs Avenue School construction cut the north-south traffic flow of Borden Avenue. It was integrated in 1946. By the time of this 1956 photograph of the eighth-grade class, the school population was nearly all African American. In 2009, the board of education voted to change the name to honor the first African American elected US president, Barack Obama. The school currently serves children in pre-Kindergarten to fifth grade. (Courtesy of Kathy Dorn Severini.)

This United Press International photograph at the intersection of Springwood and Atkins Avenues shows just one day out of four during the civil disturbance that started July 4, 1970, and lingered through July 7. The action failed to get elected city and board of education officials to address the inequalities in education, housing, and job prospects that the West Side Citizens League had brought up nearly three decades earlier in the 1940s. (Author's collection.)

Seen here is night three of a police vigil set up at 1001 Springwood Avenue, between Sylvan and Prospect Avenues. City patrolmen are, from left to right, Pat Moyna, Charlie Rockhill, Buddy Alcott, Billy Dello, Buzzy Lyons, and an unidentified officer from Middletown. (Author's collection.)

In 1973, the city council voted for a name change to Lake Avenue; the lone dissenter was Dr. Henry J. Vaccaro, who argued, "Springwood Avenue symbolizes Asbury Park as much as the Boardwalk." It would be 20 years before a new city council approved a return to the original name. New street signs went up in March 1993. Seen here in a 1998 aerial view, the corner of Springwood and Ridge Avenues at lower left was anchored by the wood-frame St. Peter Claver Roman Catholic Church that survived the disturbance, as did Mount Pisgah Baptist Church at Borden Avenue, plus a few other masonry buildings. Everything else along the avenue and many of its side streets was eventually razed; only St. Stephen AME Church was built new on the Prospect Avenue corner, but the city council turned down its proposal to build a commercial plaza that would have included a grocery store and pharmacy, citing a preference for the marketplace to drive urban renewal. These blocks continued to remain vacant until the second decade of the 21st century. (Courtesy of Kathy Dorn Severini.)

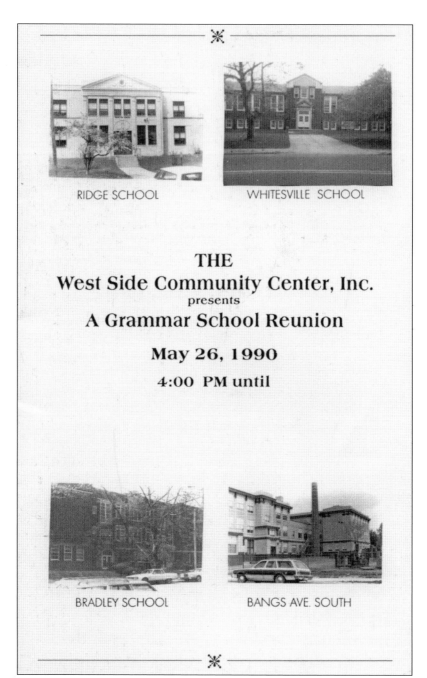

RIDGE SCHOOL

WHITESVILLE SCHOOL

THE

West Side Community Center, Inc.

presents

A Grammar School Reunion

May 26, 1990

4:00 PM until

BRADLEY SCHOOL

BANGS AVE. SOUTH

This 1990 reunion program is a poignant reminder that the West Side includes Neptune, whose border is most visually represented by the traffic line that runs down the middle of Ridge Avenue, separating the two communities. The West Side Community Center on DeWitt Avenue was incorporated as a nonprofit in 1942 as a result of the Asbury Park Urban League (founded in 1934) and the Urban League of Monmouth County (1938) "to meet the social welfare needs of Black people in Monmouth County." Before the league, local and county governments "were largely unresponsive to Black unemployment and poverty," according to the program. Co-chairs of the event were Lois Chisolm Manuel and Rainette Bannister Holimon. (Author's collection.)

Born in the city in 1926, Rainette B. Holimon (right) was the wife of police officer Percy Holimon, with whom she built a modern home on Bangs Avenue. She had a professional career that eventually took her to Iran and then on two different Peace Corps assignments to Kenya and East Africa, which became the basis of her 2001 memoir, *Reaching Out*. Here, she hosts a party for her Kenyan family, the Senessies, when they came to visit. (Courtesy of Madonna Carter Jackson.)

Rainette Holimon's early life gave her a second career in retirement, talking with students about history made on Springwood Avenue before they were born. She commissioned artist Bob Mataranglo to design a portable mural she could take into classrooms, so pupils had a visual aid in place of the daily reality of an empty avenue. The mural was unveiled at a reception at the West Side Community Center in 1999. Sadly, Holimon passed in 2017. (Author's collection.)

The late Phil Konvitz, a bail bondsman and local power broker, dabbled in real estate, buying 72 empty lots from the city after the 1970 civil disturbance. This view from 2019 shows the Springwood Avenue townhouses he built (right) and the newer dwellings built by Interfaith Neighbors (left). (Author's collection.)

Launched in 1988 to address the growing problem of homelessness, Interfaith Neighbors renovated its first home in 1998 at 1128 Monroe Avenue. From left to right are Thomas Kononowitz and Laurence M. Downes, both of NJ Natural Gas; John Marmora of Interfaith Neighbors; Mayor Carl Williams; and Tom Hayes of NJ Natural Gas. (Courtesy of Interfaith Neighbors.)

In 2006, the state Department of Community Affairs approved Interfaith Neighbors' 10-year, 60-project plan for the West Side. In 2012, the $7 million Springwood Center was completed, featuring Kula Café, a culinary training program that offers casual dining, a business development center, a police substation, and the chamber of commerce. On Atkins Avenue, the entrance to the senior center features the refurbished Turf Club neon sign, thanks to the historical society, plus entry to eight low-to-moderate-income apartments. (Author's collection.)

The Sensational Soul Cruisers, a hugely popular 11-man vocal harmony group with horns, entertains an appreciative audience in Springwood Park, the neighborhood's public square, during Music Mondays in 2019. If it rains, the Transportation Center lobby is a mere four blocks away. (Photograph by Jeri Houseworth, courtesy of Interfaith Neighbors.)

In 2016, the board of education voted to name the middle school after Rev. Martin Luther King Jr., who spoke at the high school on October 7, 1960. Its construction on Bangs Avenue near the Prospect Street intersection cut the flow of north-south traffic on Atkins Avenue as well as the east-west traffic on Mattison Avenue, even as it was built east of the Barack Obama Elementary School. The school serves pupils in grades six through eight. (Author's collection.)

The independent Sisters Academy of New Jersey is an 11-month academic program of Mercy Center, a sponsored ministry of the Sisters of Mercy, a 19th-century Irish order that established a presence in the city in 1986. Located on the southeast corner of Springwood and Ridge Avenues, the academy offers an extended day curriculum for girls in grades five through eight from not only the city, but also Neptune, Long Branch, Bradley Beach, and Brick in neighboring Ocean County. (Author's collection.)

Carolyn Curtain, seen here with Steve Albert, bought a sagging Victorian on the east side in 2002. It did not have a kitchen, so she began looking for vintage replacements. Her passion to rescue architectural artifacts grew. In 2015, she opened Salvage Angel by the Sea in the one-time Canada Dry bottling warehouse that spent its last years vacant after the Asbury Towel Co. closed on Ridge Avenue and Washington Street. (Author's collection.)

Sam and Freda Brown Aldarelli ran a hugely successful Italian restaurant they opened here at 612 Ridge Avenue in 1934. Other restaurants would come and go, including Jennie's Soul Food. This is currently the location of Masjidul Bayaan, an Islamic house of worship. (Courtesy of Steve Albert.)

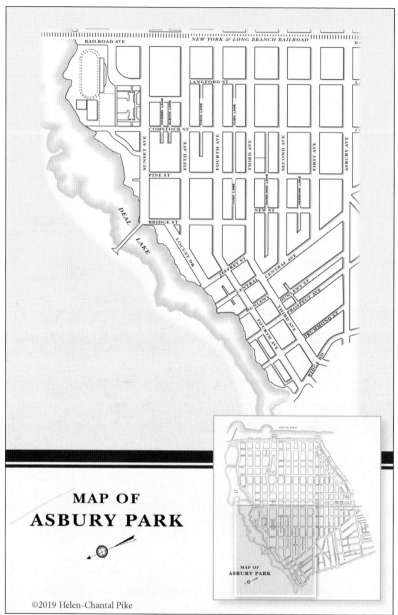

MAP OF
ASBURY PARK

MAP OF
ASBURY PARK

©2019 Helen-Chantal Pike

After Springwood, Asbury and Sunset Avenues evolved into the second and third major west-to-east corridors for routing traffic to and from the ocean. As the last tract of woodland to be developed, the northwest neighborhood retained most of the "country by the sea" character realtors promoted in the 1920s. The alleys, or lanes, north of Asbury Avenue named in 2018 pay tribute to historic addresses long-gone in the 21st century. The first three are from the southwest neighborhood (see chapter three): Kershaw's, a barbecue restaurant on Adams Street behind the Turf Club; Roseland and Cuba, two popular nightclubs on Springwood; and Fisch's, a one-story clothing store on Springwood. The fourth is a historic hotel (see chapter one). The Albion was on the north side of Second Avenue across from the Stone Pony. The last alley, Charms, honors the fruit-flavored candy that once was packaged on the southeast corner of Monroe Avenue and Heck Street (see chapter two). (Map by author.)

Four

POMP AND CIRCUMSTANCE

What a difference four decades make since the 1906 high school band photograph that was the cover of Images of America: *Asbury Park* was taken. This c. 1940s photograph in front of the "new" high school shows more African Americans and female musicians (there were none in 1906) as well as a huge variety of instruments and uniforms to perform in parades and at the all-important halftime shows during football games. (Author's collection.)

A growing year-round population of children to educate meant a new high school was long overdue. Held up by World War I, James Bradley's 1921 death, state requirements, and the need to get taxpayers to vote in favor of a $1 million bond to finance construction, the board of education finally prevailed in 1926. Ernest A. Arend, who had overseen the construction of the Bradley and Bangs Avenue Schools, worked with Newark architects Guilbert & Betelle to build a modern campus on the last available parcel that could accommodate both an academic building and outdoor playing fields: the former athletic field used by the League of American Wheelmen overlooking Deal Lake. The only other local contract went to William R. Hogg for plumbing. The dedication took place in March 1927. (Author's collection.)

In 2017, the board of education dedicated the stadium to coach William "Butch" Bruno, class of 1933. A gifted athlete and scholar who played football for Notre Dame, he returned after World War II to raise a family on Third Avenue and teach as well as coach football. He led teams to two state championships in 1940 and 1953. Another plaque honors Olympic sprinter Frank Budd, class of 1958, once billed as the "World's Fastest Human" for breaking a record in 1961. In 2005, an annual open USA Track & Field–sanctioned event was launched here in his honor. (Author's collection.)

ASBURY PARK CAVALCADE

MARCH

Dedicated to Asbury Park High School

Published by PINCUS BROTHERS — Advertising
305 Bond Street, Asbury Park, N. J.

The new athletic field and stadium had a $215,000 price tag: $65,000 for the land and $150,000 for construction. Specs called for a quarter-mile cinder running track with a 220-yard straightaway, runways and jumping pits for field events; separate soccer and hockey fields, clay tennis courts, a handball court, and an outdoor basketball court; and a playground for small children. The team mascot, the Blue Bishops, is a nod to Francis Asbury, the first bishop named to the Methodist Episcopal movement in colonial America and whom James Bradley honored by naming his residential resort after him. It also indicated how influential this Protestant church was in the city's early history. The team colors are black and blue. Advertising men Sidney and Irving Pincus put a 1946 copyright on this booster song written at the end of World War II. The chamber of commerce used the cavalcade theme for its annual trade show in ConHall until the early 1950s. For the Pincus brothers, there was not much other than a mention of Sidney as the advertising manager for Tradio, makers of coin-operated radios for hotels operated out of the 900 block of Sunset Avenue in 1949. That facility was the last address of Anthony Sammarco's Asbury Syrup business, which supplied restaurants and boardwalk concessions started by his father as Manhattan Club Beverages. (Author's collection.)

Bob and Doris Carroll moved east from Freehold in 1962 with their six children, buying a large, rambling bungalow on Sunset. Anticipating the 1980s renaissance, the couple mapped out a plan for a community newspaper in their living room. When the *New York Daily News* offered Bob a buyout, he took it to work full-time running the *Coaster*, which they had launched in 1983 with their sons Tom and Rob and daughter Ellen, its current editor. The *Coaster* office is on the west side of Main Street between Third and Second Avenues. (Author's collection.)

In 1901, Albert Robbins took over the real estate business of a city pioneer, William H. Beegle, at 226 Main Street. As the northwest neighborhood began to be developed in the 1920s, Robbins opened a home office at 805 Sunset Avenue. When he died in 1930, his realty firm was taken over by William H. Warren, a fellow Rotarian. (Author's collection.)

Booted from General Motors, which he had founded, Willy Durant in 1921 launched a new automobile line under his own name and opened a showroom on Railroad Avenue, between Fifth and Fourth Avenues, while living at his sumptuous estate, Raymere, in Deal. But he died a pauper after declaring personal bankruptcy in 1936. He was last seen, according to the January 2007 issue of *Hemmings Classic Car*, washing dishes at a burger stand attached to a grocery store converted from part of the Durant showroom seen in the center of this late 1930s photograph. He died in 1947. Handsomely renovated into a shopping plaza in 2016, the building is known as the Shops at Sunset Point. (Author's collection.)

To date, the only known female real estate developer in the city was Clara Augusta Smock Saunders, wife of Albert Saunders. Together, they raised two sons on Fifth Avenue, and she oversaw the construction of two rental bungalows at 915 Fifth Avenue, now a condominium complex marketed under the name Mallory Square. Born in Howell in 1897, she died in Ardmore, Pennsylvania, in 1984 and is buried in Mount Prospect Cemetery in Neptune. (Author's collection.)

George and Patricia Fischer pose with their children Frank and Mary Pat for a 1950s family portrait with the miniature Fischer Baking Company delivery truck used as a kiddie ride in the Bubble Land Express Train Ride, the mechanized amusements on the Boardwalk at the foot of First Avenue operated by Robert Fountain. (Courtesy of Mary Pat Fischer.)

Three brothers took their mother's humble cake shop and turned it into Fischer Baking Company in Newark. In 1930, a branch was opened in Asbury Park on Railroad Avenue between Fifth and Fourth Avenues. With other locations in the New York metro area, the string of commercial bakeries was sold in 1962 to Bakery Enterprises Inc. After a series of owners, the firm went bankrupt in 1966, leaving 200 employees in Asbury Park without a job. The building was later converted into county government offices, including social security. Later still, it was used as a warehouse. In 2020, it was in the early stages of a multi-unit residential conversion. (Author's collection.)

Henry Smock Conrow turned his skill at carpentry into a talent for architecture, working for his relations at Buchanon & Smock Lumber. For 17 years, he lived in Asbury Park, building this home on Fourth Avenue before moving to Kansas. In 2005, Steve Albert and Lou Liberatore bought the converted two-family residence that had been covered in yellow asbestos shingles, and Steve lovingly began to return the asymmetrical Victorian to its original glory as a single-family home. (Courtesy of Steve Albert.)

In the north, Mayor Frank "Boss" Hague ran Jersey City; in the south, Atlantic County sheriff Nucky Johnson ran Atlantic City. Monmouth County sheriff and mayor Clarence E.F. Hetrick ran Asbury Park. Highly recommended is chapter two in the 2009 book by Joe Bilby and Harry Zieglar, *Asbury Park: A Brief History*. The mayor built himself a fine home on Fourth Avenue, complete with a stained glass window featuring the letter H. (Courtesy of Steve Albert.)

Finding the medical field too crowded in the gold-rush town of Victor, Colorado, Dr. Harry Thomas headed east after learning about the flourishing residential resort. He and his wife settled on this Fourth Avenue house where his son, adventurer, travel writer, and radio pioneer Lowell Thomas, came home to write his most enduring work, *With Lawrence in Arabia*, about the World War I British spymaster. The book was released in 1924. (Courtesy of Steve Albert.)

Having lost their original location at Asbury Avenue and Pine Street to fire in 1945, West Asbury Park Methodists moved deeper into the developing northwest neighborhood. The new redbrick Ballard United Methodist Church went up on Fourth Avenue near the Dunlewy Street extension. (Author's collection.)

In 2019, Third Avenue resident Jen Souder let her dining room be turned into a recording studio for the Asbury Park African-American Music Project with councilman Yvonne Clayton. With the support of the library, the historical society, and the Bruce Springsteen Archives & Center for American Music at Monmouth University, the all-volunteer group's mission is to record the oral histories of musicians who experienced the city's music heritage. (Courtesy of the Asbury Park African-American Music Project.)

In 1999, Third Avenue resident and retired police captain Rashid Khan (left), along with Charles Harris of Neptune (right), created a Civil War reenactors' group to portray the regiment of black army volunteers from New Jersey who organized as the 22nd US Colored Troops Infantry Regiment in 1864. For a number of years, their group participated in various parades and other public events in New Jersey, including this one on April 13, 2003, at the Peter Mott House in Lawnside, Camden County, to commemorate the start of the Civil War. The troop has since disbanded. (Photograph by Hoag Levins.)

The original 1907 grammar school named for James A. Bradley was segregated, with many African American pupils in the northwest neighborhood sent to Bangs Avenue School (see chapter three), to accommodate white students from the districts of Allenhurst and Interlaken. Since torn down, its replacement is an integrated elementary school with an expanded Third Avenue campus from Pine Street east to Comstock Street. The property's west side is bordered by the alley Roseland Lane. Bradley Elementary School serves pupils in pre-Kindergarten to fifth grade. (Courtesy of Steve Albert.)

In 2015, longtime board of education photographer and instructor Angel Kames opened the Cuban Café with business partners Roberto Perez and Dunechky Hernandez, all of whom have family ties to Cuba. They made over the checkered drive-through on Memorial Drive that occupies a corner of the parking lot for the city's only remaining grocery store, Super Supermarket (formerly Grand Union). This block was once part of the sprawling Buchanon & Smock lumber yard. (Courtesy of Susan L. Rosenberg.)

In 2010, Berkshire Hathaway Home Services purchased the Buchanon & Smock Lumber Co. on Second Avenue and Langford Street from Henry Vaccaro Sr. and retrofitted the former industrial site into the Lofts. Vaccaro operated a number of businesses here, including Vaccaro Guitar. For a brief time, he warehoused Michael Jackson memorabilia here, the result of a lawsuit from a missed payment by the Jackson family for their purchase of his Kramer Guitar Company. (Courtesy of Steve Albert.)

Returning west and past Bridge Street, realtors promoted a "Bungalow Neighborhood" around Locust Drive that included the Minot House. Son of a sea captain who owned a fashionable 19th-century hotel on the oceanfront, Jesse Minot chose to build his home in this more wooded enclave near a finger of Deal Lake. A longtime officer in the Asbury Park and Ocean Grove Bank on Main Street, he later became a founding officer of the Red Bank Trust Co. and died in Fair Haven in 1933. (Courtesy of Steve Albert.)

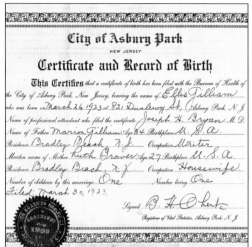

Trained as a midwife, Mary Meyers Gunther of Johnstown, Pennsylvania, in 1922 built a 12-room house in the 800 block of Dunlewy Street. Seven of the rooms were bedrooms where women could give birth and convalesce. Maternity cottages played a critical role in helping women of modest means give birth safely. Gunther operated the Gunther Nursing Home until 1941. (Left, courtesy of Steve Albert; right, courtesy of Ellis Gilliam.)

Asbury Park High School alum and former Marine Ellis Gilliam knew the city better than most and spent a lot of time at the library responding to research queries. Growing up, his family moved twice a year based on his father's salary and the fluctuating rates of seasonal rentals. Ellis made a copy of his birth certificate as proof of where he had been born, on March 26, 1923. He died in 2006. (Courtesy of Jessica Varian-Carroll.)

Dubbed Horner's Corner, where Dunlewy meets Asbury Avenue, city police officer Howard Horner and his wife, Olive, took over a drive-in eatery Celia Brown had opened in the early 1930s but closed in 1937. The couple lived two doors east at 1307 Asbury Avenue. Their married daughter Doris H. Garrabrandt ran it until she retired in 1975. The mention of pork barbecue sandwiches, milk floats, and orange drinks continues to stir passionate food memories. It is now the Light of the World Apostolic Faith Church, where Pastor Astley Stewart Sr. and first lady Gloria Stewart welcome parishioners. (Courtesy of Susan L. Rosenberg.)

After operating a successful wholesale produce business started by his immigrant father in 1928, Giacoma "Jimmy" Marrucca and his wife, Diane, took over the former Freddie's Pizzeria between Prospect Avenue and Drummond Street and opened Jimmy's Restaurant in 1982. Using their knowledge of fresh produce, they created a menu of flavorful Italian dishes. Jimmy passed in 1992, but Diane continues to run the highly regarded dining spot. (Courtesy of Steve Albert.)

The Order of the Sons of Italy was established in 1905 to help Italian immigrants assimilate in urban areas in the United States. In 1911, the Order Sons of Italy in America Grand Lodge of New Jersey was established. Long closed as successive generations moved out to the suburbs, this was the Sons of Italy building on Asbury Avenue near Ridge Avenue. (Courtesy of Steve Albert.)

When it closed its doors, Asbury Park Mount Carmel Lodge 1215 Sons of Italy gifted this bust of Christopher Columbus to the public library. The successor organization, with its inclusion of women and emphasis on families, is the charitable Italian American Association of the Township of Ocean, where heritage and culture are celebrated, not assimilated. (Author's collection.)

A seemingly massive masonry building, the Methodist Episcopal Church was built in 1916 by missionary Methodists who regarded the neighborhood surrounding Asbury Avenue as "Hell's Kitchen." It was destroyed by fire in 1945, and the property was sold to the expanding Italian Catholic population looking to move Our Lady of Mount Carmel from its cramped sanctuary on Bangs Avenue. (Author's collection.)

In 2010, a process began to combine four historically ethnic Catholic churches founded between 1881 and 1981: Our Lady of Mount Carmel (Italian), Holy Spirit (Irish), St. Peter Claver (African American), and Our Lady of Providence (Haitian, in Neptune). The new Mother of Mercy Parish is under the direction of the Fathers of the Society of the Divine Word, founded by Fr. Arnold Janssen in the Netherlands in 1875. (Author's collection.)

Umberto Grieco arrived from Italy in 1925. By the end of the decade, the barber who would also become a state boxing inspector had established a Republican political club for Italian Americans. In 1943, the Umberto Grieco Political Association dedicated its new Progressive Club on Asbury Avenue at Comstock Street. Edward A. West was club president. (Author's collection.)

In the wake of the 1970 civil disturbance, the Improved Benevolent and Protective Order of Elks of the World lost their clubhouse on Adams Street (a block south of Springwood). The J.T. Newman Lodge No. 998 and Elizabeth Bunn Temple No. 667 eventually moved into the former Italian American clubhouse on Asbury Avenue. This photograph was taken around 2000. (Author's collection.)

After Springwood Avenue, the next west-east transportation corridor to develop was Asbury Avenue. Not only was it important for making deliveries into the residential resort, it was, and still is, the political artery to the Monmouth County seat of Freehold and farther west to state offices in the capital of Trenton. This aerial view is from 1998. (Courtesy of Kathy Dorn Severini.)

Welcome "Boardwalkers"

FROM THE

CITY OF ASBURY PARK

WISHING YOU EVERY SUCCESS ON YOUR

1966-67 SEASON · · ·

ANOTHER SPORTING
SPECTACULAR FROM THE
FAMOUS CONVENTION HALL

ASBURY PARK

WHERE EVERYTHING'S NEW BUT THE OCEAN

A GREAT PLACE TO LIVE — WORK — PLAY

FRANK H. ROWLAND, Mayor

COUNCILMEN

Ascenzio R. Albarelli   Edward R. English

Joseph F. Mattice   Henry J. Vaccaro, M.D.

City Manager Paul H. Hermann

A few decades before there was the Shore Cats basketball team (see chapter two), there was the Boardwalkers of the Eastern Professional Basketball League. The investors—Paul Larson of Larson Ford GM in Wall Township and Richard S. Sambol of Sambol Construction, Toms River—bought the defunct Cambria-Johnstown franchise in Pennsylvania and moved the team to Asbury Park, where it would play in ConHall, according to the *Red Bank Register*. To the returning players was added six-foot-five newcomer Walt Mischler, APHS class of 1958, who had played freshman basketball in high school and for the Boys Club. The genial Mischler also distinguished himself at Monmouth College by leading the country's small colleges in rebounding and shooting his senior year. The Boardwalkers coach was Larry Hennessey of Neptune High School. The Boardwalkers lasted one more year after this 1966–1967 tourist guide book was published before the franchise was moved to Massachusetts and renamed the Springfield Hall of Famers. (Author's collection.)

Five

CODA

Religion continues to have a significant presence in Asbury Park. When the dwindling Asbury Park Wheelmen members could no longer sustain their second clubhouse on the northeast corner of Grand and Sewall Avenues, in the 1940s, St. George Greek Orthodox Church took over the lot, razed the building, and in 1949, built a magnificent sanctuary. When plans to build a spacious religious campus in suburban Ocean Township were completed in 2012, the edifice was used by the ReVision Theater, which moved from the Casino carousel house for its fifth season. About 2013, the Ministerio Internacional La Senda, a member of the Hispanic Assemblies of God, moved in, led by Pastor Roberto Arias. Despite a Grand Avenue address, the doors open on Sewall, where ironically, across the street was the Prince of Peace First Hispanic Presbyterian Church, itself built on the site of the Dutch Reformed or Grand Avenue Reformed Church. Prince of Peace moved to Matawan, making way for the 28 South Grand townhomes developed by K. Hovnanian around 2015. (Author's collection.)

The 200 block of Cookman Avenue had been the fabled address not only of the Palace Amusements (see chapter two), but also of Walter Reade's Lyric Theatre, where he experimented with television broadcasting in that industry's infancy. The theater ended its days as the Park Cinema, an adult movie house. Most of this block is a parking lot and the current site of Tandem Cycle, an indoor cycling studio built by iStar that opened in 2019. (Author's collection.)

Built by the Kushner Companies (see chapter one), the Wesley Grove condos replaced two quirky triangular blocks and their streets originally laid out in 1870 to match the contours of Wesley Lake. The redesign of streets along with the elimination of landmark buildings will make it increasingly difficult to identify historical scenes and addresses in the decades to come. (Author's collection.)

East of the movie house, the Talking Bird Café and Sands Hotel was a late-night eatery and short-term lodging run by Ed Schau and his partner of 60 years, Carmen DiFilippantonio. It was, recalled Frank D'Alessandro, a "place where folks of all ages and genders could find refuge." In 1991, the city's first pride parade—about a block long, according to Frank—paid tribute to "the boys" as it marched past the beloved address. The following year, Asbury Park became the annual site of the Jersey Pride Parade that kicks off Pride Month in the Garden State on the first Sunday in June. The pair sold their property to Kushner and moved to Las Vegas before retiring to Delaware. (Author's collection.)

An artist for the now-defunct Road Ad Sign Co., Leslie W. Thomas designed Tillie for the Palace expansion on Cookman Avenue in 1956. He borrowed from the iconic face used to promote the Steeplechase on the northwest corner of Ocean and Second Avenues that was lost to fire in 1940. "Funny Face" was one of 125 artifacts salvaged by Save Tillie, aided by Baumgartner Construction of Egg Harbor, in 2004 before the Palace came down. Tillie was placed in the sewer authority's parking lot. (Author's collection.)

Manager of Fischer's Bakery (see chapter four), Frank Fiorentino was mayor during one of the more difficult periods of municipal history, from 1982 to 1989. He is seen here happily presiding over the event that annually signals summer will arrive soon: the Easter parade. In 1985 or 1986, he congratulates the winner of Most Stylishly Dressed Woman, Carol Best Holmes. (Author's collection.)

In 2013, the chamber of commerce paid tribute to the more than 30 years of volunteerism by photographer Ken Roth by naming the Kenneth T. Roth Landmark Business Award after him. He is seen front and center (with glasses) at the third annual beer can swap he helped organize in ConHall in 1979. (Author's collection.)

THIRD ANNUAL EAST COAST BEER CAN SWAP
JUNE 1979 JERSEY SHORE CHAPTER

Though nameless now, he once worked in Creative Services at the Steinbach Department Store, either designing print advertisements or decorating windows, or both. Whether he was the same artist who frequented the Cameo Bar (see chapter four) or not, he did paint this backdrop in the bathroom of the home where he lived at the Santander on Deal Lake Drive and Park Avenue. (Photograph by Milton Edelman, author's collection.)

Toddy Hoyt's Red Coats were local musicians who played the Monterey Hotel in the summer of 1930. From left to right are (first row) Roy Walter, alto sax; Frank Branin, tenor sax and clarinet; Hoyt, banjo; and Earl Pyle, violin and tenor sax; (second row) Joe Bartlett, trombone; Fred Smith, drums and alto sax; Ed McDonald, bass horn; and Bill Crawford, piano. In the summer of 1942, Johnny Johnson and His Orchestra, featuring Nina Orla, performed nightly in the White Jungle from 10:00 p.m. until 1:00 a.m. (Author's collection.)

In 1939, John R. Wolter, a member of the Asbury Park Fishing Club, wrote the words and music to the song *Freedom in the Good Old U.S.A.* Merchants advertised on the back cover. Bold type at the bottom promoted Potter's Barbershop and Beauty Parlor at 617 Mattison Avenue. For more about rock and folk music pioneers Margaret and Tom Potter, read *For Music's Sake: Asbury Park's Upstage Club and Green Mermaid Café. The Untold Stories* by his granddaughter Carrie Potter-Devening, published in 2011. (Author's collection.)

Garwood antiques dealer Richard Yorkowitz bought the shoe-store-turned-music-club-turned-footwear retailer in 2009 for $1 million. But Hurricane Sandy in 2012 disrupted his plans to make over the property. In 2015, brothers Jim and Bill Ross paid $650,000 for the property on the southwest corner of Cookman Avenue and Bond Street, and by February 2020 were well on their way to putting a new façade and interior on the three-story building that will have four apartments, plus ground-floor retail. The Thom McAn sign painted on the building's rear side will remain. (Author's collection.)

With a lot of his Asbury Park property heavily mortgaged and undeveloped, an ailing James Bradley died at 91 on June 6, 1921. He was buried in the Gillespie Mausoleum in Woodlawn Cemetery in the Bronx, New York, where his wife, Helen Packard Bradley, was laid to rest in 1915. The family crypt was probably built initially for her nephew Louis Packard Gillespie, who died in 1905. His father, Louis C. Gillespie, was in the import-export business of varnishes, gum, and oil. Bradley's death marked the end of an era. (Author's collection.)

DISCOVER THOUSANDS OF LOCAL HISTORY BOOKS FEATURING MILLIONS OF VINTAGE IMAGES

Arcadia Publishing, the leading local history publisher in the United States, is committed to making history accessible and meaningful through publishing books that celebrate and preserve the heritage of America's people and places.

Find more books like this at
www.arcadiapublishing.com

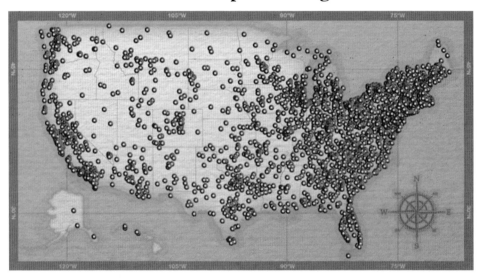

Search for your hometown history, your old stomping grounds, and even your favorite sports team.